POCKET BOOKS

Also by *Dr. Bob Rotella*

Golf Is a Game of Confidence
The Golf of Your Dreams
Putting Out of Your Mind
Life Is Not a Game of Perfect

GOLF IS NOT A GAME OF PERFECT

DR. BOB ROTELLA

with Bob Cullen

POCKET
BOOKS

This edition first published by Pocket Books, 2004
An imprint of Simon & Schuster UK Ltd
A CBS COMPANY

14

Simon & Schuster UK Ltd
1st Floor
222 Gray's Inn Road
London WC1X 8HB

www.simonandschuster.co.uk

Simon & Schuster Australia
Sydney

A CIP catalogue record for this book
is available from the British Library

ISBN-13:978-0-7434-9247-8

Printed and bound in Great Britain by
CPI Group (UK) Ltd, Croydon, CR0 4YY

Foreword to the British Edition

I WAS PARTICULARLY PLEASED TO LEARN THAT THERE WOULD BE A BRITISH edition of *Golf Is Not a Game of Perfect* so that more golfers from these isles could get to know Bob Rotella's unique and down-to-earth brand of mental fitness.

I have worked with Bob for many years and while he has helped to remind me of some of the timeless lessons of golf, he always does so with a fresh eye and a clear focus on what matters most. There are countless 'mind-doctors' and 'gurus' on the tour who spend a lot of time dressing up conventional wisdom and complicating common-sense. Bob Rotella is the real deal, whose virtue is to keep it simple so that I can do the same on the golf-course.

Golf Is Not a Game of Perfect has been one of the most-thumbed books in my golfing library for a long time. I understand that it was originally written nearly ten years ago but the lessons contained within are as important today as they have ever been. Staying positive, overcoming your fear of failure, setting yourself the right goals, avoiding those fatal lapses of concentration and focusing on the next shot instead of the last one are all crucial ways of improving your score, and all are covered here in a really accessible no-nonsense manner.

For most of us, when things aren't going well, rebuilding our swing or changing our putting style is not an option. Nor should it be. A reminder of the basic mental exercises, which the Doc explains so well, goes a long way towards turning things around.

Darren Clarke
March 2004

Introduction

Over the past thirteen years, I've been fortunate enough to work with many of the greatest golfers in the world. This book is an effort to share with others who love the game what I've taught some very successful golfers and what they've taught me.

The psychology of great golf is quite plain and logical. Most players with whom I work are at first amazed by the simplicity of what I tell them. They're surprised to find that there is nothing weird or mysterious in what I do. With a bit of relief in their voices, they tell me that the type of thinking I teach strikes them as good common sense.

Sport psychology, as I teach it, is about learning to think in the most effective and efficient way possible every day. It's the psychology of excellence. My job as a coach of mental skills is to help players go where they might not be able to go on their own, given their old ways of thinking.

They may have learned ways of thinking that work on a driving range or a practice green. What I offer is a way of thinking and playing that works under the fire of competitive pressure, that breeds consistency, provides the best chance to "go low," and helps players find a way to win.

The challenge lies not in understanding the concepts I teach, for, as I've said, they're simple and make common sense. The challenge lies in thinking this way every day on every shot.

To meet this challenge, golfers must understand the power within themselves. They must learn to tap this power and let it flow into their golf game.

One of my goals in writing this book is to expose people who love golf to the truth about free will. I am convinced that it is the power of will that separates great golfers from those who never reach their potential.

Though I teach psychology, I have never known for sure where the mind ends and where heart, soul, courage and the human spirit begin. But I do know that it is somewhere in this nexus of mind and spirit, which we call free will, that all great champions find the strength to dream their destinies and to honor their commitments to excellence. All great champions are strong on the inside.

They all learn that competitive golf either builds character or reveals character. They learn to be honest about their thoughts. They learn to relish the game's mental and emotional challenges. They learn to appreciate the value of thinking in an athletic manner. Finally, they learn that golf is a game, and it has to be played.

I also know that it's all too easy, in this age of videotape, for the media to overlook the role of the mind. Television cameras can't take pictures of thoughts. But anyone who plays championship golf will tell you that at least half the battle occurs inside the golfer's mind.

This book will equip you for that challenge. Because I think it's important to learn from the experience of other players, I've drawn lots of illustrations from the history of the game and from conversations I've had with the players I teach. I hope these anecdotes will help readers understand and remember the principles I want to convey. They are the honest truth about golfing excellence.

Read and enjoy.

Contents

Foreword

....

By Tom Kite

THROUGHOUT THE YEARS, THERE HAS BEEN A GREAT DEAL OF DISCUS-sion about the game of golf and about improving scores. Invariably, the discussion turns into a debate on exactly how much of the game is physical and how much is mental. Generally, the better a player is, the higher the percentage he will attribute to the mental side. That's reasonable. A beginner, who has very little control over his swing, can't be expected to understand that the game is 80 percent or 90 percent mental. But on the PGA Tour, where all the players can hit quality shots, the mental side is at least 90 percent of the margin between winners and losers. Percentages aside, no matter what a player's handicap, the scores will always be lower if the golfer thinks well.

There have been untold thousands of instruction books written on golf. Most have chapters on the grip, the stance, posture, swing plane, alignment, and the rest of the game's mechanics.

But, given the mental side of the game's importance, far too little has been written on it. There must be reasons for this. Maybe it's because it's impossible to see what a person is thinking. Many times I have had fans tell me how cool I looked on the course, when all I could remember was how scared or nervous I had been. Or, possibly, it's because the top players, those who have found an effective way to think on the course, are very protective of any thoughts that might aid an opponent. Or maybe it's because few people have studied the mental side of golf compared with the vast number who have studied the swing. But for whatever reason, accurate information on the mental side of the game is long overdue. Bob Rotella's book—this book—is it.

I met Doc in 1984 at the Doral Open in Miami. I was in one of those phases where I just couldn't seem to do anything right on the course, and my scores showed it. I hadn't had a top finish for months, and winning a tournament seemed as far away as the moon. But after a couple of meetings early in the week, when Doc did no more than refresh my memory of those great thoughts I usually have when I am playing my best, I went out and actually won the tournament, beating none other than Jack Nicklaus down the stretch. My swing hadn't changed at all in the couple of days since the last event. But I was like a new person. All of a sudden, I could hit shots that I could not even imagine the week before. My patience level increased dramatically. Even my walk was confident. I had a new best friend, and it was me!

In the first twelve years of my life on the PGA Tour, I had established myself as a pretty decent player but had only won five official tournaments. In the ten years since meeting Doc, I have won fourteen tournaments, played on the Ryder Cup team, and won my first major, the U.S. Open. To say that I think Doc has helped make me a better player would be an understatement. I now realize that I must spend as much time working on a good mental approach as I do hitting balls on the practice tee.

But don't let the idea of yet another task scare you! This won't require much hard work on your part. After all, we all have thoughts running through our minds all the time. What Doc can do is show you what thoughts are advantageous and what thoughts are destructive. And one of the really neat things that comes along when you try this approach is that not only do you become a better golfer, athlete, or sales executive, but you learn more about yourself and become a more fulfilled person.

Who says we can't have it all?

1.

....

On *My* Interpretation

of Dreams

....
....
....

I HAVE TWO things in common with Sigmund Freud. I have a couch in my consulting room. And I ask people to tell me about their dreams. But there the resemblance ends.

The couch is in my basement rec room, near the Grounds of the University of Virginia in Charlottesville. The picture frames above it hold not the psychoanalyst's carefully neutral art but a print of a golfer swinging a mid-iron and a flag from the 18th hole at Pebble Beach, signed by Jack Nicklaus, Tom Watson and Tom Kite. A four-and-one-quarter-inch putting cup, sunk into the floor, and a universal gym complete the decor. And no one lies on my couch. They sit, and we talk face to face.

Freud believed dreams were a window into the subconscious mind. From them, he spun a web of theory that, too often, boils down to a belief that people are the victims of circumstances beyond their control—of childhood traumas, parental mistakes, and instinctive impulses.

But the dreams I ask about are not the ones that crept from the unconscious the night before. They are the goals and aspirations a golfer has been carrying around in his or her conscious mind.

The dreams I want to hear of excite some fortunate people from the time they wake up each morning until they fall asleep at night. They are the stuff of passion and tenacity. They might be defined as goals, but goals so bright that no one need write them down to remember them. In fact, the hard task for the professionals I work with is not recalling their dreams, but occasionally putting them out of their minds and taking some time off from their pursuit of them. The dreams I want to hear about are the emotional fuel that helps people take control of their lives and be what they want to be. Time and again, I have heard stories of dreams that are intimately connected to the ability to play great golf. In fact, this is the first mental principle a golfer must learn:

A person with great dreams can achieve great things.

A person with small dreams, or a person without the confidence to pursue his or her dreams, has consigned himself or herself to a life of frustration and mediocrity.

PAT BRADLEY HAD some of the most exciting dreams I have ever heard. When I first met her, in the early 1980s, she had won a number of tournaments, but she wasn't convinced she knew how to win. She wasn't even sure she was innately gifted at golf. As a kid, she had concentrated most of her attention on skiing. She hadn't won many important amateur events, and she hadn't attended a college with a great women's golf team. She was a good player who just slowly and gradually got better, until she was making a good living as a professional.

She sat on my couch and said, "I'm past thirty. I want to win more. I want to win majors. I want to be Player of the Year at least once. And I want to be in the LPGA Hall of Fame."

At that point, I didn't even know what it took to get into the LPGA Hall of Fame. I quickly learned that, in all of sports, it's the hardest Hall of Fame to enter. A golfer has to win thirty tournaments, at least one of them a major. Very few make it.

I said to myself, "Wow. This woman has a great head."

Just talking with her exhilarated me. She was so intense and so excited. She had a quest.

We worked for two days on how she could learn to see herself as a winner, to think effectively, to play one shot at a time, to believe in her putting and herself. We talked periodically thereafter, and still do.

The first year after our visit, she won five tournaments, three of them majors. She nearly won the Grand Slam of women's golf. I attended the one major she lost that year, the U.S. Women's Open in Dayton, Ohio. She lipped out putts on two of the last three holes and lost by a shot or two.

Afterward, we talked, and I told her I was glad I hadn't been carrying a million dollars with me, because I would have bet it all on her to win the Open. That was how impressive her attitude and confidence were that year.

Pat continued to win, and in 1991, with her fourth victory that year, she qualified for the LPGA Hall of Fame. The induction ceremony was at the Ritz-Carlton in Boston, and Pat invited my wife, Darlene, and me. We came into the lobby and saw Pat and her mother, Kathleen. We exchanged hugs.

"Hey, before you leave, we have to talk," she said.

"What do we need to talk about?" I asked.

She looked at me and said, "Where do we go from here? Bob, we've got to find a new dream. What's next?"

Pat is still trying to figure out what comes next. For a while, she thought that the 1996 Olympics would include golf and be played at Augusta National. She had always dreamed of playing at Augusta, and she had always dreamed of being an Olympian. The prospect of doing both fired her up, until the International Olympic Committee dropped the idea.

Now she's searching for a new dream. And she hasn't won since 1991. I know that when she seizes on a new dream, she will win again. Her dreams propel her.

I HEARD SOMETHING similar from Byron Nelson recently. Tom Kite and I were giving a clinic at Las Colinas Country Club, outside of Dallas, and we were flattered that Byron and his wife, Peggy, showed up to listen to what we had to say.

After our presentation, during the question period, Byron raised his hand.

"People have often asked me where my mind was the year I won eleven tournaments in a row," he said. "I've never had a good answer, until now, when I listened to what you and Tom were saying about going after your dreams.

"When I was a young player, my dream was to own a ranch. Golf was the only way I was going to get that ranch. And every tournament I played in, I was going after a piece of it. First I had to buy some property. Then I had to fence it. Then I had to build a house for it. Then furnish the house. Then I had to build barns and corrals. Then animals. Then I had to hire someone to look after it while I was touring. Then I had to put enough money aside to take care of it forever.

"That was what I won tournaments for. It's amazing, but once

I got that ranch all paid for, I pretty much stopped playing. I was all but done as a competitive player."

Tom Kite is a great example of a person who dreamed huge dreams, and kept dreaming them in the face of all kinds of supposed evidence that they were foolish.

A few years ago I was down at the Austin Country Club working with Tom the week before the Tournament of Champions. He had to go inside to take a phone call, and while I waited for him to return, a tall, athletic-looking man walked up to me and introduced myself.

"You're Bob Rotella, aren't you?" he asked. "What are you talking to Kite about? You know, he really thinks you're helping him."

We shook hands, and he identified himself as an old friend and competitor of Tom's from boyhood days.

"I went to high school with Tom and played golf with him," the man said. "Ben Crenshaw was right behind us. Ben won the state championship twice. I won it once. Tom never won it. I thought I was way better than him. He seemed to be always shooting three over par. How did he get so good?"

There was a long answer and a short answer to that question.

The short answer was that Tom had a dream and he never stopped chasing it.

As a boy, he was small, needed glasses, and wasn't even the best junior golfer at his club. His dream seemed so unlikely that when he was fourteen or fifteen, his parents took him to see Lionel and Jay Hebert, the former touring pros. Tom's father wanted the Hebert brothers to tell Tom something discouraging, to tell him how high the odds were against him.

The Heberts, fortunately, demurred. "He'll find out soon enough how hard it is," they said. "Let him go after it."

When Tom and I first met, dreams still motivated him. He wanted to win more tournaments, including majors. He wanted to be player of the year. He wanted to be the leading money winner.

He has fulfilled those dreams. Now he has new ones. Two days after he won the U.S. Open for the first time, he called me up. He knew what would happen when he returned to the Tour. Everyone he met would want to congratulate him. Reporters would want to interview him about the Open. Fans would mob him. Faced with those distractions, a lot of new Open champions have suffered letdowns. Tom was determined not to be one of them. He wanted to test his self-discipline. He wanted to be a player who used the Open as a springboard to even better performance. And he did.

I suspect Tom will attain his new dreams as he did the old ones, because he has always been willing to do what was entailed in the long answer to the question posed by his boyhood rival.

The long answer would have recounted how hard Tom worked, on both the physical and mental aspects of his game, how often he endured failures, how often he bounced back, as he pursued those dreams.

The man I was speaking with had made a common mistake in assessing Tom. He confused golfing potential with certain physical characteristics. Most people carry in their mind an image of a golfer with potential. He is young, tall and lean. He moves with the grace of the natural athlete and probably has excelled at every sport he's ever tried. He can hit the ball over the fence at the end of the practice range.

But while I certainly wouldn't discourage someone with those physical characteristics, I've found that they have little to do with real golfing potential.

Golfing potential depends primarily on a player's attitude, on how well he plays with the wedges and the putter, and on how well he thinks.

It's nice when Tom gives me a little of the credit for his achievements, but the truth is that he had a great attitude before I ever met him. He had a backyard green and sand trap as a boy, where he developed his short game. He refused to believe he couldn't achieve his goals. Those qualities of mind were and are true talent and true potential. I believe that with his mind and attitude, if Tom had decided as a five-year-old that he wanted to be a great basketball player instead of a great golfer, he would have been an All-American in basketball. That's because talent and potential have much more to do with what's inside an athlete's head than with his physical characteristics.

I'm sometimes asked if there is a distinct champion's personality. I see no evidence that there is, because the champions I've worked with cover a broad spectrum of personality types. They come from cities and small towns, poverty and wealth, athletic parents and nonathletic parents. Some are shy and some are gregarious. Tom Kite and Nick Price, if they were in law and accounting instead of in golf, might well find they had few common interests.

But they and other champions all have a few common characteristics. They are all strong-willed, they all have dreams, and they all make a long-term commitment to pursue those dreams.

In fact, I think it's often more difficult for a person branded with what most people perceive as potential to become great than it was for, say, Pat Bradley.

When everyone around you is telling you you have great potential, and they expect you to win all the time, you can quickly start to hate and despise the potential you have, to perceive it as a burden. Val Skinner, one of the players I work with on the LPGA Tour, has struggled with that problem. She came to the tour as the Collegiate Player of the Year, and she hits it a long way. When she didn't win immediately, she got frustrated and critical of herself. She's had to work hard to realize that her physical talent is only one factor in her golfing ability—and not the most important factor.

Most people use only a small percentage of their innate physical ability, anyway. The golfer whose attitude enables him to tap a higher percentage of a relatively modest store of God-given talent can and will beat the one who doesn't know how to maximize what he has.

ON THE OTHER hand, a player with no dreams has little real potential. Not too long ago, a young man from another university came to Charlottesville to see me, looking for help with his golf game. I asked him what his dreams were.

"I don't know," he said. "I'm a pretty talented golfer, a pretty talented student. I do pretty well at both. My dad's got a pretty good company, and I guess after college I can go to work for him and make a pretty good living, so I'm not worried about the future."

The conversation floundered for a while. Finally I asked if there was anything he really loved doing, anything that truly excited him. He perked up immediately.

"Oh, yeah! I love going to see our school play basketball. The team is so awesome, so good, so into it. They're like on a mission, Doc. I'd stay up all night in a tent to get tickets to the games. I go on the road with them."

His school indeed had a successful basketball program. The team had been to the Final Four several times.

I stopped him and told him, "I don't want to break your heart, but you must realize that if your school's golf program was as good as its basketball program, you couldn't play."

He asked why.

"You have talent, but your school recruits basketball players with both talent and attitude," I said. "Your basketball coach dreams of winning national championships. He recruits only players who are totally committed to winning national championships. If you're not, he doesn't want you. Because if you're not, you're not going to work on free throws every day until you become an excellent free-throw shooter. If you're not, you're not going to play defense every night."

Free throws and defense, I said, are like the short game in golf. They require not so much talent as determination and commitment. And they are usually what separates teams that win national championships from aggregations of slam-dunk artists.

I asked how many times that year his golf coach had talked about winning the national championship.

"Not at all," the boy replied. In fact, the team had felt it did very well just to qualify for the NCAA tournament, where it failed to make the cut. They had a party after the tournament was over.

"That's the point," I said. "You have to look at what you're aiming for, because that's going to influence your level of commitment. I guarantee you that guys on your golf team practice when they want to practice. I guarantee that they spend all of their time on the range working on their swings and that no one's ever over at the practice green working on the short game. And I bet most of you spend a lot of time justifying being so-so golfers because you're at a very demanding school, academically, and you spend too much time studying."

He nodded.

I told him it would be harder for him to achieve great things in golf than it would be for his school's basketball players to achieve great things in their sport, because he would have to do it himself. He would have to set his own goals higher than his team's, and commit himself to achvieving them. It would be an individual quest, and sometimes a lonely one.

THAT'S BECAUSE THE world is full of people happy to tell you that your dreams are unrealistic, that you don't have the talent to realize them.

I never do that. Whenever someone introduces me or identifies me as a shrink, I am tempted to correct him. I'm not a shrink. I'm an enlarger. I am not in the business of telling people that they don't have talent, that their dreams are foolish and unnattainable. I want to support people's talent. I believe in human abilities.

If someone came to me and said, "I'm forty-five years old, my handicap is 25, and my dream is to make a living on the Senior Tour," I would say, "Fantastic! You're just the kind of person who excites the living daylights out of me. Just the fact that you're shooting 95 and you're talking about being able to shoot 70 every day means you have the kind of mind that has a chance. I live to work with people like you."

I would not guarantee this fictitious duffer more than a chance. The next question would be whether he could keep that dream in front of him for eight or fifteen years. The right thinking can quickly and substantially lower the score of any golfer who has been thinking poorly. But there is no rapid, miraculous way to go from a 25 handicap to scratch, no matter how well a golfer starts to think. Improvement takes patience, persistence and practice.

If a golfer chooses to go after greatness, whether he defines greatness as winning the U.S. Open or winning the championship at his club, he must understand that he will encounter frustration and disappointment along the way. Tom Kite played in and lost more than a dozen U.S. Opens before he finally won one. Big improvements require working and chipping away for years. A golfer has to learn to enjoy the process of striving to improve.

That process, not the end result, enriches life. I want the people I work with to wake up every morning excited, because every day is another opportunity to chase their dreams. I want them to come to the end of their days with smiles on their faces, knowing that they did all they could with what they had.

That's one reason golf is a great game. It gives people that opportunity.

2.

....

What Nick Price Learned
from William James

....
....
....

SEVERAL YEARS AGO, Nick Price came to see me for the first time. I met him at the airport and we drove to my home.

Nick was then in his early thirties. He was a good professional, but not a great one. He had not won a tournament in six years and had never won a major.

He had dreams. He dreamed of winning all the major championships. And his talent was apparent in the very low numbers he sometimes posted—rounds in the mid-sixties and lower.

But he was capable of following a 64 with a 76 and shooting himself out of a tournament. Inconsistency plagued him.

As we talked, it became apparent that Nick had a problem shared by a lot of professionals. His thinking depended on how he played the first few holes. If they went well, he fell into a relaxed, confident and focused frame of mind. Not coincidentally, he shot an excellent round. But if the first few holes went poorly, his concentration was shattered. He might start trying to fix his swing in the middle of the round and become increasingly erratic.

The worst thing that could happen to him, he said, was to hit his approach shot close to the pin on the first hole. If he then missed the putt, he became discouraged and timid. He putted worse. This was the state of mind that accounted for the all-too-frequent 76.

Nick let events control the way he thought, rather than taking control of his thoughts and using them to influence events.

"If you're going to be a victim of the first few holes," I said, "you don't have a prayer. You're like a puppet. You let the first few holes jerk your strings and tell you how you're going to feel and how you're going to think.

"You're going to have to learn to think consistently if you want to score consistently," I went on. "You wouldn't be foolish enough to try a different swing on every shot, would you?"

No, he said.

"It's the same way with your mind," I said. "You're going to have to decide before the round starts how you're going to think, and do it on every shot. You have to choose to think well."

NOT MANY PEOPLE think that their state of mind is a matter of choice. But I believe it is.

Unfortunately, major branches of psychology and psychiatry during this century have helped promote the notion that we are all in some sense victims—victims of insensitive parents, victims of poverty, victims of abuse, victims of implacable genes. Our state of mind, therefore, is someone else's responsibility. This kind of psychology is very appealing to many academics. It gives them endless opportunities to pretend they know what makes an individual miserable and unsuccessful. It appeals as well to a lot of unhappy people. It gives them an excuse for their misery. It permits them to evade the responsibility for their own lives.

But I didn't get into psychology through the normal academic route. I got in via the back door, from the gym. I grew up in Rutland, Vermont, where my father owned a barber shop. As a boy, I wanted nothing more than to play. I played football, basketball and baseball at Mt. St. Joseph Academy in Rutland. I played basketball and lacrosse at Castleton State College, and did well enough that the school recently inducted me into its Hall of Fame.

Golf, then, was only a minor interest. In the summer I carried clubs at the Rutland Country Club, where a neighborhood friend of mine, Joe Gauthier, was caddy master. I played a few rounds a year, on Mondays, just because my friends were doing it.

By the time I became a teenager, coaching fascinated me. I liked to hang around coaches and listen to what they had to say. I was blessed by contact with some excellent mentors. My cousin, Sal Soma, was one of the greatest high-school football coaches in New York state history. He was a good friend of Vince Lombardi, and I hung on every word he said about training and motivating athletes. My next-door neighbor, Bob Gilliam, coached basketball at Kimball Union Academy in New Hampshire. He impressed me with how much fun he had developing a team and getting the players to believe in themselves. My elementary-school basketball coach, Joe Bizzarro, taught me that the team that wins is usually the one that believes in itself. My entire high school experience at Mt. St. Joseph was filled with invaluable lessons. Jim Browne, my high-school basketball coach, was an extremely talented player and coach from Ridge-field Park, New Jersey, who had survived the Korean War. He taught mental and physical toughness; one of his drills cost me a front tooth. But I remember not caring because I loved his approach to the game. Tony Zingali, an assistant football coach who was the backbone of a legendary high-school program, taught us that we had to be mentally disciplined every day in practice if we wanted to be disciplined on game days and that attitude would always win out over ability. My quarterback coach, Funzie Cioffi, who had played for Lombardi at Fordham, passed along the necessity of having and executing a game plan. Bill Merrill, the head baseball coach at Castleton State, lived in my dormitory. We talked for hours about coaching. He taught me that if an athlete or a team wanted to be successful, a way could be found. He proved it with his baseball team. Roy Hill, one of my basketball coaches at Castleton, taught me that an athlete had to stay focused at all times and that the size of your heart was far more important than the size of your body.

I started to coach informally when I was in college. At Christmas break one year, the basketball squad was told that every Friday afternoon it would be working with a busload of retarded children from a nearby institution called the Brandon Training School. I thought, at first, that the basketball team could hardly afford to waste practice time working with retarded kids. But after a while, I started to enjoy doing it. Those youngsters would happily try anything we wanted to teach them—dribbling, shooting, an obstacle course, or tumbling. They always had good attitudes. They were always in good moods.

The varsity athletes I played with had almost everything going right in their lives. They were good-looking, talented guys. But a lot of them focused on the little things that were wrong with their lives. They wanted to be taller, or they wished their families had more money.

In contrast, these retarded kids had almost everything going wrong in their lives. But they focused on the only thing that was going right—their chance to learn to play. And they learned, despite their limitations. It started to hit me that attitude, self-perception and motivation heavily influenced success in life. I realized that happiness had more to do with what you did with what you had than with what you had.

After college, I continued teaching the retarded; and Frank Bizzarro, the brother of my elementary-school basketball coach, gave me a job as an assistant coach at my old high school in Rutland. The more I coached, the more convinced I became that the Xs and Os that obsessed many coaches were rather less important than the attitudes and confidence they instilled in their players. Without confidence, concentration, and composure, teams lose. With confidence, almost any plays would work. So when the chance came to go to graduate school at the University of Connecticut, coach lacrosse at the university and basketball at the university high school, and pursue a degree in sports psychology, I took it. Eventually, I got my doctorate and became director of sports psychology at the University of Virginia. Since 1976, I've had the enormous pleasure of working with the University's athletes in all sports.

As a psychology student, I soon found myself skeptical of a lot of the theories and theorists I read. For one thing, a lot of the theorists were themselves unhappy individuals. I was attracted, on the other hand, to the ideas of people who seemed to have a knack for happiness and success. In particular, I liked the ideas of William James, the most prominent American psychologist of the nineteenth century. Once, at a meeting of the

American Psychological Association, James was asked to identify the most important finding of the first half-century of university research into the workings of the mind. His reply became part of my philosophy:

People by and large become what they think about themselves.

The idea is so simple that it is easy to dismiss. People become what they think about themselves. It's almost all a person needs to know about how to be happy.

If someone came to me and asked me how to be happy, I would reply that it's simple. Just wake up every morning thinking about the wonderful things you are going to do that day. Go to sleep every night thinking about the wonderful events of the past day and the wonderful things you will do tomorrow. Anyone who does that will be happy.

John Wooden, who won nine national basketball championships at UCLA, expressed the same idea; maybe he'd also read William James. Winners and losers, Wooden said, are self-determined. But only the winners are willing to admit it.

That strikes a lot of people as fatuous. But it's quite realistic if you accept another old concept that has unfortunately gone out of style: free will.

I harp on free will with the players I work with. Free will means that a person can think any way he or she wants to think. He can choose to be a happy person or a miserable person. She can choose to think of herself as a great golfer or a born loser.

Free will is the greatest gift anyone could have given us. It means we can, in a real sense, control our own lives.

On the golf course, it means that a player can choose to think about his ball flying true to the pin, or veering into the woods. She can choose whether to think about making a putt or just getting it close.

Every now and then a player says to me something like, "Doc,

I just involuntarily started thinking about hitting the ball into the water. I couldn't do anything about it."

My response is, "No. You can indeed do something about it. You can think about the ball going to the target."

A golfer can and must decide how he will think.

IN NICK PRICE'S case, these ideas meant that Nick could choose to allow a few missed early putts to affect his thinking for an entire round. Or he could choose to think the way he did when those first few putts dropped and he was on his way to a 64. He could think only about what he wanted to achieve on the course, about the ball going to the targets he would select. He could think about scoring well insead of real or imagined flaws in his swing or his putting stroke.

After listening to this for a while, Nick said, "If I had known this is what you were going to talk about, I would have come to see you a long time ago."

"Why didn't you?" I asked.

"Well," he replied, "I was afraid you'd be into something weird. I didn't realize it would be this logical and sensible."

I laughed. At that point, Nick and I were ready to go out to the practice tee and work on how he could control his thoughts and make his game more consistent.

3.

Train It and Trust It

GOLFERS LIKE TOM Kite, Pat Bradley and Nick Price have come to me with exciting dreams and aspirations. But they have encountered obstacles, and they want help overcoming them. A lot of them tell me that they've never worked harder practicing their game, but they're not getting better scores. Almost all of them want help learning to win and to play more consistently.

The high handicappers whom I see in clinics tend to be people tying themselves in knots, physically and mentally. They've read all the books and all the golf magazines and they've been to six different pros, and they can't understand why their games aren't more consistent. Or they say that they hit the ball well on the range, but not on the course.

But, pro or amateur, whatever their specific concerns are, they all know one thing. They're better players than they're showing on the golf course and in tournaments.

This raises one of the essential issues in golf. Why is it that a golfer cannot simply command his body to repeat the motion that has brought success thousands of times on the practice range or the putting green?

The answer has to do with connections between the brain and other parts of the nervous system that we still only vaguely understand.

Having come to golf from other sports, I bring a broader perspective than that of professionals who have devoted their entire careers to the mechanics of the swing. To me, the act of striking a golf ball belongs in that category of sports events in which the player need not react to what another player does, as a batter must react to the pitcher. Major variables are constant and under the golfer's control—the moment the action begins, the position of the ball, and his position in relation to it. Swinging at a golf ball is, in this sense, akin to pitching a baseball, shooting a free throw in basketball, or walking a balance beam in gymnastics.

Consider the baseball pitcher. Greg Maddux of the Atlanta Braves tells me that he pitches best when he virtually forgets about the batter and thinks only of the place he intends his pitch to go, his target.

Consider the free throw. As with the tee shot in golf, nearly everything—the ball, the height of the basket, the distance—is constant, except the movement of the athlete. If you watch the best free-throw shooters, you will notice two things. First, they have routines that they follow on every shot. They may spin the ball in their hands. Then maybe they dribble the ball a precise number of times. They take their stance in the same way every time. They focus on a small piece of the rim. And they let the shot go, without giving much, if any, thought to such things as the angle formed by the right elbow at the point of release.

Or consider the balance beam. If you lay a four-by-four-inch beam on the floor and ask people to walk from one end to the other, it's easy. Most people will instinctively focus their vision and attention on the far end of the beam, their target. And they will walk confidently and casually until they reach it.

Now mount the beam forty feet in the air, with no net underneath. Physically, the task remains the same as it was when the beam was on the floor. Mentally, though, it has changed dramatically. Mounting the beam high in the air introduces a strong fear of failure.

Most people, in such circumstances, will respond by starting to think about mechanical things they didn't worry about when the beam was on the floor. How, exactly, does a person keep his balance? And how does he put one foot in front of the other? Toes in or toes out? Body sideways or facing straight ahead? Eyes on the end of the beam or on the feet? Arms limp or extended to the sides? Their goal will become not falling, rather than getting to the end of the beam. They will stop trusting the body's ability to remain balanced as they negotiate the distance. Thinking that way causes the muscles to tighten and the movement of the body to grow spasmodic and jerky rather than rhythmic and graceful. If you actually conducted the experiment, many people who successfully negotiated the beam when it was on the floor would fall off from forty feet.

In much the same way, a golfer who fears failure—as most amateurs and many professionals do, at least some of the time —tends to think about how he takes the club back, how far he turns, how he cocks his wrists, how he starts the downswing, or other swing mechanics. Inevitably, he will tend to lose whatever grace and rhythm nature has endowed him with, which leads to inconsistent shotmaking with every club, from the driver to the putter.

This suggests a most important principle:

You cannot hit a golf ball consistently well if you think about the mechanics of your swing as you play.

When someone asks me why this is so, I cannot give a scientific reply. Psychologists and other specialists in human performance may one day figure it out. I simply know that the human organism performs a task like the golf swing much better if the athlete looks at a target and reacts rather than looks, thinks and reacts. I don't want to impose religion on anyone, but the only explanation I can come up with for this is that someone created us this way. We are endowed with the most marvelous computer system imaginable, and it is wired to maximize physical performance and grace if a person simply looks at a target and reacts to it.

There is, of course, a time and place for thinking about the mechanics of the golf swing. I am not one of those who try to sell the notion that golf is purely mental and that mechanics don't matter. They do. It is much better to have a good swing than a bad swing. To be successful, a golfer must blend work on mechanics with work on the mental approach to the game. The professional golfers I work with all have swing teachers who help them with their mechanics.

But the time to worry about swing mechanics must be limited, and the place to worry about them is the practice tee and only the practice tee. If you step onto the course with the intention of shooting your best possible score, you cannot think about mechanics. On the golf course, you have to be like the good free-throw shooter who eyes the basket and lets the ball go. You have to be like the person who walks across the balance beam without thinking about how to walk. You have to believe that you've practiced the golf swing enough to have faith in it. To put it concisely:

✓*A golfer must train his swing and then trust it.*

When I say this at clinics, someone usually stands up and says that trusting the swing might be all well and good for a Tom Kite or a Nick Price, who has endless hours to practice and who hits the ball almost perfectly almost all of the time. But how can a weekend player who sprays the ball all over the course trust his swing?

I respond that I have seen lots of high handicappers with lots of kinks in their swings, but I almost never see one who improves his play by doubting himself, dwelling on mechanics or trying to correct a swing flaw in the middle of a round. The fact is, most amateurs don't know exactly what breaks down when they swing badly. If they try to correct their swing, they usually wind up compounding the error. They would be far better off forgetting about their swing mechanics, thinking about appropriate targets and strategy, and making up their mind that they will shoot the best score possible with the swing they brought to the course that day.

Yet, this notion of trusting the swing strikes many weekend players as difficult, if not impossible. But how often have they hit the ball well while thinking of mechanics? Why do they fear abandoning the effort to control and guide their swing?

It's just habit, habit that has become comfortable, however ineffective.

The fact is that neither Tom Kite nor Nick Price nor anyone else I work with hits the ball perfectly or even close to perfectly all the time. In fact, over the past ten years I've been working regularly with players who have posted well over two hundred and fifty wins on the PGA Tour, LPGA Tour, and Senior Tour. I can't remember more than a few times when a winning player has told me he or she hit the ball really well for more than two of the four days of a tournament.

Winners learn to accept the swing they bring to the golf course on any given day and to score with it. They win tournaments, as often as not, because they manage to use their short game and their mind to avoid a high round on the day or days when their swing is not what they wanted. If they need to work on their mechanics, they do it after the round is over, or they take a week off and go to the practice tee.

Even Jack Nicklaus had limits in his ability to repair a faulty swing on the course. Tom Kite told me about a round he and Nicklaus played during the PGA Championship. Nicklaus split the fairway with his driver on the first hole. On the second hole, a short par four, he used a 3-wood. The third was a par three. On the fourth hole, he pulled out his driver, but he pull-hooked the ball, almost out of bounds. Tom said it was the worst shot he'd ever seen Nicklaus hit. From that moment until the end of the round, the driver stayed in Jack's bag, even though the championship was being played at Kemper Lakes, a brutally long, 7,200-yard course. Despite its length, Nicklaus played it with the clubs he could trust, his 3-wood and his 1-iron. He saved the driver for the practice tee after the round, where he drove balls until he was satisfied he had worked out the kink that had produced the pull-hook at the fourth hole.

Most golfers, amateur or pro, lack Nicklaus's patience and discipline. Most of them would react to a pull-hook like the one Nicklaus hit on the fourth tee that day by taking the driver out on the next tee and trying to fix their mechanics. They'd start thinking about how fast their hips opened, or when they turned their hands over, or their swing planes. And their score would suffer for it.

Trusting is not instinctive or easy for most golfers. They experience it only sporadically. Maybe they have a club that gives them such a feeling of confidence that they can trust their swing when they use it. They get better results with this club because trust allows them to swing decisively and fluidly. This reinforces their confidence with that particular club. Or they feel trust in the midst of a hot streak.

The challenge, of course, is to trust your swing with every club and score well when your shots are telling you that your swing is not in the slot. It's not easy or instinctive for many people. But this is the way great golfers and all great athletes think.

This was the way Tom Watson played in his prime. The worse he hit it, the more he ripped it. He knew that if he reacted to a bad shot by getting more careful, it would not make his swing better. It would make it tentative—and worse. I've seen him hit it seventy yards left, then seventy yards right and then hit the third one screaming on line to the pin.

At the Nabisco Championships a few years ago, Chip Beck, whom I was working with, shot 63 on Sunday. It was a big breakthrough for him. He had a chance to win if Watson faltered behind him.

Watson could barely put the ball on the golf course down the stretch, but he kept getting up and down. On the last hole, he had a 6-iron approach to a tiny green surrounded by trees, with the pin cut tight to one side. But he knew what to do. Just as he always did, it was one waggle, two waggles, and let it go. And he knocked it stiff. That's why he's been a great player. He knows that no matter what happens, he has to keep trusting. He's gotten away from that in recent years with his putter, but I always expect him to come back, because he knows how to think the way great athletes think.

When great athletes stop trusting, they stop being great. The difference in a player's attitude can be very subtle. A little doubt or a little indecision is sufficient to impair performance.

When great players are playing well, trust becomes a habit. The golfer executes his shots without being aware that he's trusting his swing. He simply picks out a target, envisions the kind of shot he wants to hit, and hits it. Brad Faxon will often hit a draw off the tee on one hole and a fade on the next, depending on the shape of the hole. But he tells me that he never thinks about the mechanics of a draw or fade. He trusts that his body will produce the swing needed for the shot he envisions.

If you don't trust right now, you will have to go through a period of conscious awareness until you learn the difference between the feeling of trust and the absence of trust. You will have to work at developing thoughts and habits that promote trust. You will have to learn to focus your mind on your target and your preshot routine rather than on swing mechanics.

How Stuart Anderson Created His Own Reality

FINE ATHLETES IN every sport know the importance of trusting their mechanical skills. And they do it regardless of the results they achieved on their last attempt.

One of the best stories on the subject that I've ever heard came from Stuart Anderson, a University of Virginia football player who went on to play for several years with the Washington Redskins. Stuart took a seminar I gave on confidence in athletics. I asked him to share with the class what went through his mind when he was thinking confidently.

Stuart replied with a story from his high-school basketball career.

"I was a fifty percent shooter from the floor," he said. "In the first round of the state playoffs during my senior year, I took my first shot and I missed."

Stuart kept missing. He had the worst shooting night of his

life in that game. He missed twenty-odd shots in a row. His team teetered on the edge of elimination.

One of the other students in the seminar asked, "Stuart, why didn't you start passing the ball after you missed, say, ten in a row?"

"Because I'm a shooter. But let me finish the story," Stuart said.

His team scrapped and stayed in the game. With a minute to go, trailing by a point, they stole the ball and called time out. The coach, reasoning that Stuart was irremediably cold that night, diagramed a play to run 55 seconds off the clock and set up a shot for another player, a junior.

"Wait a minute, Coach!" Stuart objected. "I want the shot. Give me the ball!"

The underclassman, it turned out, didn't really want the shot at that stage. So the coach, against his better judgment, changed his plan and called a play to give Stuart the shot.

He got the ball beside the free-throw line, one of his favorite spots. He turned and jumped, absolutely confident. His eyes zeroed in on the rim. He let the shot go.

And in it went. Stuart was the hero. Fans carried him off the floor. The next day, the newspapers headlined his game-winning shot.

After hearing this story, one of my students raised a hand and asked, "How did you stay confident after you missed all those shots?"

"Well, you have to understand. I've always been a fifty percent shooter," Stuart replied. "After I missed one, I figured the next one was likely to go in. After I missed two, I was overdue. By the time I'd missed five, I figured the next one absolutely had to drop. Every time I missed, I figured the odds were increasing in my favor."

"Okay," the student said. "If that's how you think when you miss your first shots, what do you think if you make your first six or seven in a row?"

"That's totally different," Stuart said. "You decide that tonight's your night, you're on a hot streak, and you're going to make everything you look at."

"That's ridiculous," the student said. "You can't have it both ways."

"Of course you can," Stuart said.

Stuart had revealed something very basic about the way good athletes think. They create their own realities. They think however they have to think to maintain their confidence and get the job done. In basketball, this is called the shooter's mentality. In golf, it's even more essential, because there is no one to come off the bench to replace a player who's struggling.

A golfer has to learn to do what Stuart Anderson did, to put aside all thought of past failures and to trust that his next swing will send his shot where he aims it. He has to develop the basketball shooter's mentality.

If he misses a few putts, he has to believe that this only enhances his chances to make the next one. If he hits a tee shot out of bounds, he has to believe that this only means he's gotten the bad swing out of his system. The shot was an accident. It's not the norm.

This may seem, to an outsider, to be absolutely irrational. How can a kid who's just missed twenty-odd shots in a row be confident he's going to make the next one?

The answer is that whether it's irrational or not, it's more effective than the alternative. Would Stuart Anderson have been more likely to make that shot if he had doubted himself? Would it have helped him to start trying to fix some real or imagined flaw in his shooting form?

Of course not. If Stuart had reacted to his missed shots by deciding that there was a kink in his shooting form and trying to fix it in the middle of the game, he would have destroyed his natural grace and rhythm. He would most likely have started shooting airballs.

Many weekend golfers don't even wait for a bad shot to stop trusting their swing. They step onto the first tee thinking of a dozen mechanical concepts they've heard from friends, read about in magazines, or seen on television. Half the time, these dozen mechanical thoughts conflict with one another. They take the driver out and start their backswing thinking about stiff left arms, still heads, full turns, wrist cocks, or pronated hands. Without realizing it, they're doing everything possible to undermine their own game.

Even the weekend players who start off trusting tend to stop doing it after a bad shot or two. They start trying to fix the mechanical problem that led to the bad shot. They would be far better off if they realized that, as human beings, they are highly unlikely to get through eighteen holes without a few bad swings. They are much more likely to play their best if they trust their swings, flawed though they sometimes are. This can be done. A golfer has free will. He can choose how he will think.

If more golfers chose to continue trusting their swings, they might be surprised at how often the brain and body respond by doing things right when it matters most—just as it happened for Stuart Anderson.

5.

The Hot Streak: Staying Out of
Your Own Way

MOST GOLFERS, EVEN mid to high handicappers, if they play often, have experienced a string of holes where everything fell into place, and for a while at least, they played the golf they had always sensed they were capable of. For one golden hour, perhaps two, the golf ball went where they wanted it to go and they strung together pars. Then something happened to break the spell—an errant tee shot, a stubbed chip, a three-putt green. They went back to making bogeys. Perhaps they thought that during the hot streak they played over their head.

They did not. The hot streak represents the golfer's true capability. It results, essentially, from trust. The golfer trusts his abilities. He steps up to the ball knowing that he can pick a target and hit it there. He does things unconsciously. The swing repeats itself. It feels effortless.

You can learn a lot from a hot streak.

I've asked many golfers to recall and describe their state of mind during their hot streaks. I have yet to hear one respond that he was thinking of swing mechanics. Most would say that the hot streak enabled them to *stop* thinking about swing mechanics. That's another way of saying they were able to trust their swings.

Players I work with have had some very low rounds and very hot tournaments. David Frost has scored 61 or 62. Nick Price shot 11 under par in a South African tournament. Davis Love III shot a 60 in Hawaii recently. Andrew Magee set the record for a 90-hole tournament in Las Vegas in 1991 with a 329, 31 under par. Tom Kite broke it two years later at Bob Hope's tournament, shooting 325.

The lowest single-round score any of my players ever recorded in an official tournament was Chip Beck's 59 a couple of years ago in Las Vegas.

Chip called me after the round, and naturally, I wanted to know as much as possible about his state of mind that day.

Of course, he had sunk a lot of birdie putts. He had hit lots of fairways and greens. Mentally, he told me, he had a serene feeling of confidence as the round progressed.

"Doc, I stayed out of my way the whole day," he said.

By "staying out of my way," Chip meant that he had not allowed doubts of any kind—particularly doubts about his mechanics—to interfere with his game. He had a plan for each hole, each shot, and he executed that plan. He trusted completely that his mechanics would enable him to do so. He let nothing from his mind interfere with his physical capabilities.

Trusting won't, by itself, turn on a hot streak. But it will make a hot streak much more likely.

If you wish to play your best golf, you can't wait until a few putts fall and a couple of birdies go on the scorecard before you start trusting. You have to start replicating the state of mind you have on a hot streak as soon as you step onto the first tee. No matter what happens during your round, you have to strive to maintain that state of mind.

You have to stay out of your own way.

6.

Rediscovering
Old Scottish Wisdom

SHORTLY AFTER I met Tom Kite, he suggested that I start regularly visting him and other players on the PGA Tour. They wanted, Tom said, to keep abreast of all the new discoveries being made in sports psychology.

I had to tell him that most of what passes for discovery in sports psychology really isn't new. There is just the same old wisdom, repeated over and over again, repackaged in new terminology.

The Scots who invented golf knew a lot of what I teach to pros today, and they passed it along to early American golfers. Bobby Jones, for instance, learned the game from a Scottish pro named Stewart Maiden at the East Lake course of the Atlanta Athletic Club, just after the turn of the century. Jones's family lived in a house near the 13th hole of this club, but as a boy, Jones did not take lessons in swing mechanics, as so many children do today. He learned the game playing around the 13th green and by tagging along behind Maiden and imitating his movements.

Jones also learned the psychology of the game from Maiden. In the midst of his great career Jones disclosed what he had been taught in his autobiography, *Down the Fairway*. Jones wrote at length about his swing mechanics in the instructional section of the book. But at the end of this section, he appended:

"One bit of earnest admonition. Stewart Maiden maintains that he cannot think of any of these details, or of any other details, during the execution of a shot—that is, if the shot is to come off. He adds that he does not believe anybody else can think of these or other details and perform a successful shot. I find this to be the case with my own play."

Other great players from American golf's early years figured this out in their own way. Walter Hagen, like Jones, learned the golf swing by imitating, though he did it as a caddie, rather than a member's son. He discovered the essential psychology of the game as a young pro, in 1914. He was working at the Country Club of Rochester, N.Y., and his game impressed the members enough that they passed the hat and paid for his train fare to Chicago, where the U.S. Open was being contested at Midlothian. Hagen, even then, had luxurious appetites. The night before the tournament began, he treated himself to a lobster dinner. But Hagen's purse was not yet commensurate with his tastes and he couldn't afford a place that served truly fresh lobster. The lobster he got was old and bad.

He awoke the next morning with a fierce case of food poisoning. He was almost doubled over with pain. Had he not been afraid of what the members back in Rochester would say if he withdrew, he would not have played. But play he did.

Because of his pain, Hagen could think only of finishing his round. He stopped worrying about the way he was swinging and thought only of putting the ball into play off the tee, getting it onto the green, and getting it in the hole.

He shot 69 and went on to win his first Open.

Sam Snead grew up poor in the hills of Virginia, and started caddying at a nearby resort. Golf fascinated him, but he had no money for clubs or lessons. He whittled sticks into the shape of clubs, found rocks for balls, and practiced in a pasture, seeing how many fence posts he could knock the rock past. Snead had a fine, intuitive sense of his own capabilities. And he soon learned that he knocked the rock farther and straighter when he cleared out his mind and just let his naturally fluid swing occur.

"I found that the best way was just to draw that stick back nice and lazy, not thinking too much about how I was doing what," Snead wrote many years later.

He had to relearn the lesson when he started playing golf professionally in the early 1930s. Snead allowed himself to be convinced that what had worked in the pasture back home wasn't good enough for professional competition. He decided he had to learn to "concentrate," which he took to mean trying very hard to swing absolutely correctly. His first tournament was in Hershey, Pa., near the chocolate factory. On the first tee of his first round, he concentrated fiercely, concentrated so hard that he thought the ball might catch fire. He sliced it into the factory grounds. He concentrated harder. Another slice, deeper into the factory grounds. He was lying four, still on the tee.

Snead's professional career might have aborted right there if he had not had the instinctive wisdom to stop trying to concentrate. He relaxed and let his body swing the club. He drove the green, 345 yards away, made the putt, and went on from there.

. . .

SOMETIME IN THE 1940s, though, American golfers began to over-emphasize and complicate swing mechanics. They began to forget the wisdom that Stewart Maiden passed along to Bobby Jones and that Walter Hagen and Sam Snead discovered for themselves. This was not, of course, true everywhere. Golf is a sport of individuals and everyone had his own approach to the game. Teachers like Harvey Penick never stopped imparting sound principles about the mental side of golf. But they became a minority.

There were many reasons for this. One, I think, was technology. As motion pictures and stop-action still photography developed, it became possible to record and study the swings of good players in minute detail. You could actually determine whether Byron Nelson pronated or supinated at the top of his backswing. Televised golf and the plethora of magazines and books reinforced the emphasis on mechanics.

Practice ranges came along, and teachers found that they could make a living just standing on the lesson tee and talking about hand positions and body coils and swing planes. They stopped walking the course with their pupils. They stopped teaching rhythm and feel and scoring skills.

Gradually, teaching golf became a big business. Teachers competed for a share of the market by claiming that they, and they alone, had discovered the secret, the mechanical key to the perfect swing. Many in the golf business fought over ownership of the "correct way" to teach the swing, even though, as it happens, almost none of the great golfers swung the club "correctly." Bobby Jones regripped the club at the top of his backswing. Walter Hagen had a forward move that resembled a lunge. Not only that, but the best players, from Jones down through Palmer, Player, Nicklaus and Trevino, have always taken pride in the fact that their swings were a bit idiosyncratic and highly personal. The best players have always had the courage to swing in their own way and ignore teachers who insisted that only a classic swing could win.

Unfortunately, as far as the mental side of the game was concerned, in the 1940s and 1950s a distorted image of Ben Hogan became the model for American golfers. Hogan was badly misperceived. The press and public saw him as a robotic exemplar of swing mechanics. In fact, as Hogan himself wrote, he played his best golf after he stopped being obsessive about swing mechanics. Until 1946, Hogan never fully trusted his swing. He played every round in fear that he could fall out of the groove. He worried about dozens of mechanical details on every stroke.

Around 1946, though, Hogan realized that he had mastered the fundamentals of the swing and didn't need to worry about them so much. He abandoned what he called "this ambitious overthoroughness" in relation to his swing. The results were dramatic. "At about the same time I began to feel that I had the stuff to play creditable golf even when I was not at my best, my shotmaking started to take on a new and more stable consistency," he wrote.

In other words, when he started to trust what he had trained, he played better.

But this was not the Hogan image. The press and the golf publishing houses presented him as a man who became great by obsessive attention to the mechanical details of the golf swing. Everyone heard how Hogan hit bucket after bucket on the practice green. Everyone heard how Hogan developed a "secret move" that cured his hook.

I had a chance to visit Hogan several years ago, and what he said differed substantially from the Hogan image.

"I played by feel," Hogan told me.

He also told me that he didn't start to win major championships until he learned that on any tough course there would always be a few holes that bothered him, where he couldn't use his driver. Once he started using 1-irons in those situations, he started to win. So strategy and course management, not perfect ball-striking, had a lot to do with his success.

A final point about Hogan makes clear the depth of the public misperception. It was brought to my attention by David Frost. Frosty is a native South African, and a couple of years ago he passed along to me an autobiography by the great South African golfer of Hogan's era, Bobby Locke. At the end of the book, Locke presented an all-star team, listing the best player he'd seen with each club in the bag. Hogan didn't make the team for ball-striking. He made it for putting.

That was so at odds with Hogan's image that I asked the great player and teaching pro Paul Runyan about it the next time Paul and I worked together at an instructional clinic. Paul confirmed that Hogan, in his prime, was as good as anybody at putts from five to fifteen feet. On the professional tour, those are the putts that separate the winners from the also-rans, because they are the putts that produce birdies.

When Hogan stopped being a confident putter and started muttering that putts should only count half a stroke, he stopped winning golf tournaments.

I wonder how American golf might have developed if someone had asked Hogan to write a book on golf psychology. Such a book might have caused people to focus, not on his mechanics, but on the nerve he showed in developing a swing that was completely different from those of his peers. It would have highlighted how he steeled his mind and refused to be distracted on the course, and how he developed the inner strength to pursue his dreams through many years of failure.

But no one ever did. And Hogan's perceived obsession with swing mechanics influenced a generation of golfers.

After Hogan, the mantle of superiority in American golf passed briefly to Arnold Palmer and then to Jack Nicklaus. Nicklaus helped reemphasize the importance of the right mental approach to the game. He was a great strategist and thinker on the golf course. He was among the first golfers to talk about visualizing the shot he desired before he swung the club. He insisted on waiting until his mind was relaxed and focused before hitting a shot.

In the past decade, thinking about golf psychology has continued to progress backward toward the wisdom of the old Scots. Jim Flick, one of the best of today's golf teachers, says that a player has to pass through three stages: unconsciously incompetent, consciously competent, and unconsciously competent.

Today's best players strive to stay on that third level. Nick Price wants to think only of his target as he swings. He tells me that he's constantly struck by how much better he swings the more sharply he focuses his mind on his target. Fred Couples says he tries to have no swing thoughts at all. They are the new avatars.

The new breed of golf winners has to have a tougher approach to the game than their predecessors did. In Hogan's day, and even in Nicklaus's, it was often sufficient to play cautiously for the first three-and-a-half days of a tournament, then cut loose on the back nine of the final round, trying to hole everything. Nowadays, winning scores are lower and players have to be free and cocky from the first hole Thursday morning. With that exception, though, not much that today's winning players say about their mental processes would surprise Stewart Maiden.

7.

What the Third Eye Sees

IF THINKING ABOUT swing mechanics can spoil a golf swing, what should a golfer think about as he stands over the ball?

A Ben Hogan story told by members of the Los Angeles Country Club suggests part of the answer. It concerns an exhibition round Hogan once played on their North Course.

Hogan came to the 5th hole, a 476-yard par five on which the green, because of the slope of the land, is not visible from the tee. A cluster of four tall palm trees, planted only a few feet apart, stands immediately behind the green and towers above the horizon.

When Hogan arrived at the tee, he asked his caddie for a target.

"Aim for the palm trees, Mr. Hogan," the caddie replied.

To which Hogan answered, "Which palm tree?"

The story is cited sometimes as an example of Hogan's perfectionism. But what it really suggests is Hogan's knowledge of one of the fundamental psychological principles in golf:

✓ *Before taking any shot, a golfer must pick out the smallest possible target.*

This may seem obvious to some people. But I'm continually amazed by the number of golfers who don't do it. When I'm at a clinic or pro-am with someone who's just sprayed his ball into the next county, I sometimes ask what he was aiming at when he hit the errant shot.

Usually, the reply is something like, "I was aiming down the left side." Or "down the middle." Or people might say, "I don't know what I was aiming at. I just knew I didn't want to miss left."

That's not good enough. Aiming down the middle is the equivalent of trying to go to Los Angeles by flying to an airport somewhere in California.

The brain and nervous system respond best when the eyes focus on the smallest possible target. Why this is so is not important. It just happens to be the way the human system works. Perhaps it has to do with the evolutionary advantage enjoyed by those cavemen who focused on the hearts of attacking tigers, as opposed to those cavemen who merely looked in the tiger's general direction and hurled their spears.

It is true in virtually every sport. We teach basketball players to look, not at the backboard, nor even the rim, but at the net loop in back of the rim. We teach quarterbacks to aim, not at the receiver, nor even his number, but at his hands.

The smaller the target, the sharper the athlete's focus, the better his concentration, and the better the results. When an athlete locks his eyes and mind onto a small target, the ball naturally tends to follow.

Satchel Paige, the old pitcher, used to put bubble gum wrappers on the edge of the plate as he warmed up. Aiming at them sharpened his control.

The small, precise target helps golfers in one obvious way, by making it easier to align the player and his club. But it has another benefit. A golfer needs to have something on his mind if he does not want thoughts about swing mechanics to intrude on his consciousness just as he is preparing to play his shot. The target helps fill that void. It helps prevent distractions.

Nick Price, after we had worked together for a while, told me that once he had picked out a target, he could look back to the ball, but continue to "see" the target in his mind. He has seen his consistency and his success greatly increase as he has committed himself to refusing to hit a shot unless his mind is locked onto the target.

Other good players tell me they feel almost as if they had a third eye on the left side of their head. Their eyes shift down to the ball before they swing. But with that third eye, they still see their target.

Tom Kite, on the other hand, looks at a small target in the distance, thinks about it, but does not see a picture of it when his eye returns to the ball. His mind is just as locked onto the target as Nick Price's. This is merely an individual variation.

Hogan was so aware of the value of a target that he told me one of the worst developments in modern golf was the demise of the shag caddie.

When he practiced, Hogan said, he always had a shag caddie stand precisely where he intended to hit the ball. This brought the target to life. The caddie wanted to field the balls with the least possible effort, catching them on the first or second hop. Hogan took pride in enabling him to do that. It made him pay attention to the target on every practice shot, in terms of both direction and distance. That habit carried over to the golf course.

On the golf course, though, finding a target is not quite so natural or instinctive as it is in, say, basketball. Off the tee, except on par-three holes, the course often presents no obvious targets. And experience, that false friend, tells you that you can't hit a driver precisely enough to bother with a specific target. So golfers are tempted to be sloppy about targets. If they fall prey to the temptation, they tend to hit, not surprisingly, sloppy shots.

Many of the players I work with have found that it's most effective to pick elevated targets—that is, something above the ground. On some courses, trees will serve this function. If you pick a tree as your target, try to focus more narrowly. Make it a specific branch on the tree. You can use a distant church steeple, a radio tower, or anything that presents something small and precise to aim for.

Only if there is no other choice, though, should you pick something like a specific undulation in a fairway. A particular point on the ground is easy to lose track of, and in the middle of your backswing, you might find yourself wondering if the undulation you looked at just before you started to swing is the same undulation you picked out when you were standing behind the ball. And good golf course architects will use undulations to create illusions that can cause you to question your alignment. That's why an elevated target is preferable.

On tee shots and full swings, your target rarely will be at the precise distance you want the ball to travel. You might aim, for instance, at a tree behind the green on a par four, knowing that you can't reach it from the tee. Frequently, your target will not be on a direct line between where your ball is and where you want it to be. A straight hitter, looking from the tee into a fairway that slopes from left to right, will pick a target to the left of center, assuming he wants the ball to wind up in the center of the fairway. He'll allow for the rightward roll he'll get once the ball hits the ground.

If you curve the ball, you need to make allowance for that when you select your targets. I'm not going to tell you that your mind can cure a slice or a hook. If you're a slicer, I don't believe you can stand on the tee, aim at a target on the right, persuade yourself that you're going to draw the ball, and miraculously cure your slice. And, of course, you now know better than to try to cure your swing flaws on the golf course.

So, work with your dominant tendency. If you normally slice the ball twenty yards off line, pick a target twenty yards to the left of where you want the ball to finish. Obviously, it's better to be able to hit the ball straight enough so that you can always aim in the fairway. But the important thing is to adjust. Too many players get obsessed with straightening out a hook or slice that they could simply play with. Without realizing it, they change their goal from shooting their best score to fixing their swing.

There's a limit to this, however. Don't ever aim at a target that would mean severe trouble if you happened to hit the ball straight. From the tee, it's all right to have a target in the rough, but not out of bounds or in a lake. And sometimes, the golf course architect will not let you aim far enough off line to correct for a slice or hook. He'll put the tee in a chute of trees, for example. In such cases, you have to go to a shorter club, one that you can hit straight enough to get out of the chute.

Many of the players I work with also pick an intermediate target on the tee to help them with alignment. This can be an old divot, a bit of paper, or the remnants of a wooden tee. All that matters is that it is precisely on the line between the ball and the target. The player picks both the target and the intermediate target as he stands behind the ball. Then he walks up to the ball with his eye on the intermediate target. He uses it to help align his clubface and his body. Then he forgets it.

Some players find the intermediate target a distraction. They prefer to align themselves using the real target. That's fine, too. Whatever you choose to do, make certain that it clears your mind and makes it easier to trust what you're doing.

LOCKING YOUR MIND onto a small target will help you deal with looming hazards. The brain tries to be an accommodating mechanism. It will try to send the ball in the direction of the last thing you look at or think about. If that happens to be a pond, you can find yourself in severe trouble. So if you're preparing to hit an approach shot over water, or a pitch over a bunker to a pin, it's important that you have an established habit of focusing your mind firmly on your target.

Most tour players have long since learned not to let things like water hazards bother them. More often, their brains get distracted by something like the flag. Fred Couples, in the final round of the 1992 Masters, barely escaped disaster when he hit his tee shot onto the bank in front of the 12th hole. Miraculously, it hung up in the grass and stayed out of Rae's Creek. Couples was able to pitch up to the green and go on to win. He later acknowledged that he had planned to play the 12th safely, by aiming for the left-center of the green. But at the last second, his attention was distracted by that siren flag, fluttering in the breeze on the right and most dangerous side of the green. Not surprisingly, the ball went where his attention did.

This is not a problem peculiar to Couples. Many players have difficulty focusing on their real target when a flag is in their field of vision. I often work with them on this, suggesting that they try to focus on something small, like a fence post in the distance, instead of a flagstick. It helps to develop the discipline they need in pressure situations.

Sometimes even the best players let a hazard distract them from their target. I went to Houston in 1986 to give a talk to some of the touring players. It was a week after the Masters. I was talking about the importance of having your mind focused tightly on the target for every shot you play. Corey Pavin raised his hand and stood up.

"That's what I didn't do at the sixteenth hole on Saturday and Sunday last week," he said.

I asked him to explain.

"Well," he said, "I'm cruising along Thursday, Friday and Saturday. I'm eight under coming into sixteen, with birdie chances ahead of me. I get up to sixteen, and for some reason I tell myself at the last second, 'Don't hit it in the water.'"

Splash.

"I go home that night," Pavin continued, "and I tell myself, 'Make sure you don't do that tomorrow.' On Sunday, I get back to eight under. I'm in position to win the thing, and I get up to sixteen, and all I can do is remember what I did yesterday and think, 'Oh, God, don't do that again today.'"

And splash again. Two mental mistakes and he was out of the hunt in the Masters.

Two things impressed me about what Pavin said. First, it confirmed one of the key attributes of the brain and how it affects your golf game. The brain, at some level, cannot seem to understand the word "don't."

If your last thought before striking the ball is "don't hit it in the pond," the brain is likely to react by telling your muscles to hit it in the pond.

That's why it's doubly important, when facing a hazard, to focus your attention sharply on your target. Obviously, you have to be aware of where the hazards are. But I tell tournament players to think about them only during practice rounds. Take the 1st hole at Augusta. It has a gaping sand trap down the right side and pines on the left. Obviously, a player wants to avoid each of them. But a player who stands on that tee, fighting nerves already, and thinks about where he doesn't want to hit it, only multiplies his chances of hitting it badly. He needs to use his practice rounds to learn where the hazards are and establish the right target for his drive—fade or draw, long or short. Then, when he steps onto the tee in competition, he must think only of that target.

The second thing that impressed me about what Pavin said was his commitment to learning about himself and his game. He didn't care what anyone else, including his peers and competitors, thought. He was intent on learning what he had to know to get better.

8.

Your Rod and Staff

WHEN TOM KITE stepped to the 18th tee at Pebble Beach on Father's Day in 1992, protecting a slim lead in the last round of the U.S. Open, it would not have been overstating things to say he faced a challenging shot.

The wind was howling. The Pacific Ocean lined the left side of the 548-yard fairway. Deep rough stood ready to punish anyone who tried to play safe by pushing the ball down the right side. Add to that the enormous pressure of being on the brink of winning a first major championship.

Bob Toski later told me that he couldn't bear to watch. Sitting at home, watching television, he had to get up and go into the kitchen, asking his wife, Lynn, to let him know what Tom did.

I was nervous as well, but I was more aware than Bob was how much Tom had practiced something that would help him handle this challenging situation.

I was not thinking of practicing drives, though Tom had certainly done that. I was thinking of Tom's preshot routine, an element of his game that he works on constantly.

A sound preshot routine is the rod and staff of the golfer under pressure, a comfort in times of affliction and challenge. It ensures that he gets set up properly, physically and mentally. It blocks out distractions. It helps him to produce his best golf under pressure.

Which is what Tom did that Sunday, smacking a 280-yard drive down the middle of the fairway.

High handicappers often tell me that what they most want to solve are problems of inconsistency. They can't figure out why what feels like the same swing produces a long, straight shot one time and a ball that fades to a splash the next.

I usually respond by asking them to describe their preshot routines. Many of them can't, because they don't have preshot routines. And yet, the pros I work with, who know the golf swing better than anyone, tell me that 80 percent of any golf shot happens before the player takes the club back: when he aims, takes his grip, addresses the ball, and, most important, focuses his mind.

This fact leads to the next fundamental principle:

The foundation of consistency is a sound preshot routine.

The next time you watch a tournament on television, take a look at a player like Tom Kite or Pat Bradley and see if you can break down his or her routine. You will find a remarkable consistency. These golfers strive to repeat the same mental and physical steps before every shot, right down to the number of waggles.

There will always be inconsistency in every golfer's results, as Kite and Bradley would be the first to attest. No one can completely prevent minute variations in the swing that can lead to great disparities in the way the ball flies. But golfers with an effective mental approach to the game know that they can control much better what happens before the swing begins, when the movements are slow, deliberate, and more susceptible to discipline. They seize that advantage by adopting a disciplined, constant preshot routine.

They use this routine for every full shot, be it a wide-open lay-up on a par five or the tightest, most challenging tee shot on the course.

Every player I work with has his or her own variation on the routine. But all sound routines incorporate certain fundamentals. A good routine enables a golfer to be trusting, decisive, and focused on the target. It fits his or her personality.

To develop a reliable routine, a golfer has to decide to follow it and practice it time after time after time until it becomes an ingrained habit that will show up no matter how much pressure he or she is under. You can be sure that under pressure, you will find out what your dominant habit is.

Some players like to begin their routines with a triggering gesture. They may fiddle with the grip on the club, or hoist the club over a shoulder. They may set a hand on the top of the driver as it rests in the bag. It doesn't matter what the gesture is. It simply serves to remind the player that his preshot routine has begun and it is time to focus intently on it. Players whose attention tends to wander on the course may find a triggering gesture particularly helpful.

Other players don't need triggers to start their routines. Just taking the club out of the bag or standing behind the ball and beginning to plan the shot suffices to get their attention. It's a matter of personal preference.

Good players feel that when their routines start, they are stepping into a bubble, a small, private world in which nothing can distract them. Tom Watson once said it feels like going into a room where everything is dim and quiet.

Once their routines are under way, most players assess the distance they want to hit the ball, the wind, the trajectory, if that's a factor, and the appropriate club. The important thing about club selection is decisiveness. If you step up to the ball still uncertain whether you have the right club, your routine is not sound. You have to start over, rethinking the shot until you are convinced you have the right club for it.

Next, pick the target. Most players do this standing behind the ball. Some do it standing next to the ball. It doesn't matter. What's important is that the target be small and precise.

This preaddress phase of the routine is the time to deal with any problems that might be caused by an unusual or unfavorable lie. If the ball is on a downslope, an upslope, or the side of a hill, take a stance next to it, take a practice swing or two, and determine the adjustments in the flex of your knees or the tilt of your shoulders you will have to make to cope with the lie. Think them through at this stage because you don't want to have them occur to you as you prepare to hit the ball. If your lie is flat, of course, this step isn't necessary.

The next step depends on the individual. Some players, when they have picked the target and club, can visualize the ball flying through the air, landing, rolling, and stopping where they want it to stop. They can visualize how their swing will look. These visions are as clear to them as if they were in a movie theater watching them.

Such visualization can help to produce a successful shot. Brad Faxon feels that the vision in his mind dictates to his nerves and muscles the type of swing to execute. If he stands on the tee of a par four that doglegs to the left and demands a high draw, he sees the high draw. That's enough to get his body to produce the swing that makes the ball fly high and curve from right to left. He doesn't have to think consciously at all about the grip, the stance, the swing plane, or any of the other mechanics that most golfers would associate with a high draw.

But you don't have to visualize. A lot of great players don't, because their minds don't work that way. They look at their targets, decide they are going to hit those targets, and how they will work the ball—draw or fade. That suffices. Some players simply focus on the target and know the ball is going there. That gets the job done.

The important thing is that you know the ball is going to the target. If you can't make yourself believe it, pick another club or another target until you can. If you've got a driver in your hands and you can't believe that the ball is going to go where you want it, put it back in the bag and take a 3-wood or an iron.

Instilling this unwavering belief in the shot is one of the fundamentals without which your routine loses its purpose. Remember that the point of the routine is not to go through a physical ritual. It is to get your body aligned properly and your mind in an effective state before every shot.

Val Skinner had an unfortunate experience at the 1994 British Women's Open that illustrates the point. Val arrived in England for the tournament a little jet-lagged, and her first-round score reflected it. But she righted herself in the next two rounds, and by Sunday afternoon, she was three under par, two shots off the lead.

On the 15th hole, though, she made a critical mistake. She drove the ball well, leaving herself an approach shot of 173 yards. There was a slight breeze. Her instinct told her to hit a 5-iron, but she chose to ask her caddie for advice. He said 6. This introduced doubt into her mind about club selection. She hit the shot with a mind infected by doubt and plugged the ball in a trap. She was fortunate to make bogey.

She repeated the mistake at No. 17. This time, her instincts told her to hit a 9-iron for a short approach shot. She asked her caddie again, and he said wedge. Again, she hit before resolving the doubt. Again, she bogeyed the hole.

She walked to the 18th tee angry. And she hit her drive in that frame of mind. It wound up in an unplayable lie, and she finished the tournament with a double-bogey. She fell from third place to ninth in the final four holes.

In each case, she later said, she failed to follow her routine. To a spectator, this would not have been apparent. Physically, she went through all the motions. But she did not follow the mental side of the routine, which required her to dispel any doubt or anger from her mind before she hit the ball.

This is often the hardest part of the routine to execute. It's not enough to go through the motions that set up the body properly. You have to set up the mind as well.

Even the best players, the ones who have learned this principle, understand it, and have practiced it, have to work constantly at it. The game is always tempting them, as it tempted Val Skinner, to hit a shot before their minds are set. Everyone succumbs to the temptation once in a while and strays from the proper routine. The best players recognize when they have done it and renew their commitment to hit shots only when they have executed each step in their mental routine.

So, NOW YOU have assessed the shot, picked the club, picked the target, and adjusted for any lie and stance variations. You may or may not have visualized the shot, but you know the ball is going to the target. Your mind is calm, focused, and decisive.

At about this point, you might want to take practice swings, particularly on shorter touch shots. Whether to take them, when to take them, and how many to take are matters of personal preference. Some of my players stand up next to the ball, take a practice swing, then go behind the ball and visualize the shot. Others prefer to visualize behind the ball, take a practice swing, and then step forward and begin their address. Still others visualize, step up to the ball and take their swings in an alignment parallel to the one they plan to use. The only important thing is that the practice swing or swings leave you feeling comfortable and decisive.

Davis Love III's routine is to visualize the shot, stand next to the ball, then take a practice swing, feeling a high draw or a high fade or whatever he's planning. His practice swing captures the feel of that shot.

The practice swing, improperly used, can inject trouble into your routine. Some people, for instance, feel it's important to take precisely the same number of practice swings before each shot. But if the last swing doesn't feel right, and they step up to the ball anyway, they can't help but have doubts about their ability to execute the shot. They would be better off being flexible about the number of practice swings they take, making certain that the last one feels right and inspires trust in the swing.

Some of the best players are inconsistent about practice swings. Brad Faxon sometimes takes a full practice swing. Sometimes he takes merely an extended waggle. Sometimes he does nothing at all. He knows that the purpose of the routine is not to take a certain number of practice swings, but to set him up properly, mentally and physically, for the shot. So he does what feels right at the time.

The practice swing can be the back door through which

thoughts about swing mechanics invade your routine. Many players, as they take their practice swings, remind themselves of all sorts of mechanical concepts, from keeping their heads still to following through. It is difficult, perhaps impossible, for them to then step up to the ball and banish those thoughts from their minds.

I much prefer that a player take his practice swing with his focus on the target, thinking only of loosening up, feeling the right swing and gaining confidence.

I know that many golfers cannot easily bring themselves to do that. They go through a phase where they simply must think about mechanics on the practice swing. If you fall into that category, my advice is to take at least two practice swings. Let the first one be the one on which you think about mechanics. Once your mechanics feel right, take a final practice swing in which you concentrate only on target and feel.

In the ideal routine, the player takes his grip and his stance unconsciously and correctly. I like to see my players take their grip while they are standing behind the ball, rather than during their address. I don't want to see them fiddling with the grip over the ball.

The best professionals can deal with their grip and stance unconsciously because they recognize their importance and they practice them, sometimes more than they practice hitting golf balls. Many of them have full-length mirrors at home on which they have placed tape to indicate where their hands, shoulders and other checkpoints should be when they set up properly.

Amateurs may not be able to spend as much time on this as professionals, or they may find it boring, but it's still a good idea. The correct grip and stance are so important that if you plan on taking only one golf lesson for the rest of your life, I would recommend that it deal only with grip, stance, alignment, ball position, and developing a routine that enables you to mentally and physically set up properly every time.

Until you reach the stage where you can unconsciously take care of grip, stance, and alignment, you need to be consciously meticulous about your setup. As soon as you've completed setting up, shift gears mentally, stop thinking about mechanics, and focus on the target.

Then the most important part of an exemplary routine begins. It's deceptively simple:

✓ *Look at the target, look at the ball, and swing.*

The idea that underlies this fundamental principle is the same one behind trusting your swing. Your brain and body work best together when the brain reacts to a target. Once you have completed your setup and locked onto your target, further delay can only be an opportunity for unwanted thoughts and distractions to disturb your concentration and pollute that pure and unconscious reaction.

You will, however, see some professionals who spend a long time with their eyes focused on the ball after they have taken their last look at the target. Jack Nicklaus did this. If it works, it is a sign that the player doing it has a highly disciplined mind. But I wouldn't teach any beginner, or any golfer just developing a routine, to stand over the ball very long once that final look at the target has been taken.

Of course, you don't want to rush your backswing. Your routine at this stage should have a pace that fits your personality, yet has rhythm and flow: Look at the target. Pause. Look at the ball. Pause. Swing.

This core of the routine remains the same for all shots, from drives to putts.

Some players have faster natural rhythm than others. Nick

Price is most effective with a pace that would feel rushed to Davis Love or David Frost. A player has to find a tempo that feels right to him or her.

Individual routines also vary on such things as waggles. Tom Kite has for years had a routine that incorporates several looks and waggles after the address. It works for him and I wouldn't recommend that he try to change it. Tom does the most important thing very well. After his last look at his target, he starts the swing without delay, his mind focused narrowly on his target.

One of the first things I look for when a player I'm working with is having trouble under pressure is the rhythm of this final part of the routine. If the time between the last look at the target and the beginning of the backswing grows any longer on the course than it was on the practice tee, that's a sure sign that the player is not maintaining his or her routine.

UP UNTIL THIS point, most golfers find everything about this pre-shot routine intuitively satisfying. Then it strikes them that there is no place in it for a swing thought. And they panic.

The best swing thought is no swing thought. But I understand that most golfers have been raised with them. So if a player tells me he absolutely must have a swing thought, I let him have one.

But he can have only one per round, and only for shots of 120 yards and longer. Switching from one swing thought to another bogs the mind down hopelessly in mechanics. And from 120 yards and in, it's important that nothing interferes with concentration on distance and the target, on getting the ball into the hole.

Some swing thoughts are more conducive to staying focused on the target and trusting your mechanics than others. "Nice and slow" is a good swing thought. Counting your looks and waggles is a good swing thought.

The swing thought should suggest an effortless motion. There is a big difference, mentally, between "Take it back straight" and "Make sure to make a really straight takeway." The former is flowing and effortless. The latter is so tight, careful and contrived that it's deadly.

The same is true of almost any swing thought that involves the downswing. Once that club starts forward, you're courting disaster if you try to think about its path and control it.

YOU CAN'T ALLOW yourself to be rushed through any segment of your preshot routine. But a player with a sound and deliberate preshot routine need not be a slow player. In fact, a person with a sound, deliberate routine should be a faster player, because he or she will spend less time in the woods looking for lost balls. And he or she won't spend long chunks of time frozen over the ball, reviewing all the mechanics that someone has said must be executed perfectly.

I advise my professional players to make their routines as short and simple as possible. The best routines are often the simplest and take the least time. It's easier to repeat a simple routine than a long, complex one.

I also advise them to make sure they can execute their routines well within the time allowed by the rules, so that they never need worry about a slow-play penalty.

I never urge a professional to hasten his routine unless I see evidence that indecision, rather than being deliberate, is the cause of the slowness. This happened recently with a young player I've been working with, Glen Day.

Glen was having the best tournament of his rookie season at the Anheuser-Busch Classic in Williamsburg, Va. He had the lead after 36 holes. But then he began playing very slowly. The television network covering the tournament made an issue of it, superimposing a clock on the screen as soon as it was Glen's turn to play. He shot 72 and fell out of the lead.

He called me after the third round, upset about the added pressure this placed on him. I sympathized with him. It's not something the network would probably have done to Jack Nicklaus. But Nicklaus has the wherewithal to retaliate against a televison director who offends him. A rookie doesn't. This, I told Glen, was a fact of life he would just have to put up with.

Then I told him that he had another, better reason to speed things up. When he and I had worked on his routine, he had no trouble making his shots within the time allotted by the rules. But in the tournament, once he got the lead, he started having trouble making up his mind. He read putts two and three times. He changed clubs before approach shots. That was taking up time. More important, it was undermining his confidence. It showed in his score. I told him he ought to trust his first instinct on putts and club selection the next day.

He did, and though he finished second to Mark McCumber, Glen shot 66 and Mark had to sink a couple of great pitch shots on the final holes to beat him.

There is a distinction between being indecisive at the beginning of the routine and being distracted close to the end of the routine. While I want my players to be decisive, a player should never hit a shot if he is distracted and not absolutely ready. If this means backing away from the ball and starting the routine over again, so be it.

This was a point I emphasized to David Frost when we started working together a number of years ago. Frosty thereupon went on to New England for a tournament and called me after the first round.

"Doc, I had to back off from about ten shots today," he said.

"What happened?"

"Well, one time I heard a baby crying. Another time someone jingled change in his pocket. Another time the wind kicked up. But you told me not to hit the ball if my mind wasn't where it should be, and I walked away every time. Should I have had to do it that often?"

"What," I asked, "did you shoot?"

"Sixty-six," David replied.

"I guess you did," I said.

I assured him he would not always have to walk away so often. As his routine became an ingrained habit, he would be less prone to distraction. But the most important thing was that he had played a round free of mental errors, where in the past he probably would have hit two or three bad shots because of lost concentration.

The main reason I see for slow play among amateurs is not players following deliberate routines. Nor is it players who back away occasionally when they are distracted. Slow play may be caused by three types of golfers. People who aren't ready to play when it's their turn because they're too busy chatting, or watching their friends hit, are slow. Indecisive players, second-guessing their club selection, are slow. Players who give themselves swing lessons as they address the ball are slow.

You can begin a sound routine while the other members of your group are hitting their shots. You can figure the yardage and pull the club. You can read the green while others are putting. If you have an unusual lie, you can assess it and take a few practice swings while you're waiting. Then, when it's your turn, you're immediately ready to focus on the target, believe in the shot, set up, look at the target, look at the ball, and swing.

I believe amateurs, even more so than professionals, ought to trust their first instincts regarding club selection or the break of a putt. If your first thought as you walk up to an approach shot is "5-iron," you will be better off ninety-nine times out of a hundred if you hit the 5-iron decisively, rather than waffle about using a 6. If your first thought on a putt is "right lip," you will be better off hitting it there than if you start to consider whether that spike mark six feet from the hole is going to throw your ball off line.

If you do these things and develop a sound, simple routine, you will find that even if you occasionally walk away and restart your routine because something has interfered with your concentration, you will be a faster player.

9.

Let the Short Game Flow

ONCE IN A while, I come across a player I don't help to improve. Almost invariably, this is a player who cannot accept the fact that low scores depend on how well a golfer plays once the ball is within about 120 yards of the hole. This is a player who persists in thinking that golf is about who hits the longest drives or the prettiest 3-irons.

It's not. Everything that happens from the tee to that 120-yard range is almost insignificant compared with what happens thereafter. In fact, I'll occasionally tell a player that I don't care what he does with his long game—whether he focuses on a target and follows a routine or not—as long as he tries what I suggest about wedging, chipping and putting.

A good golfer must not only accept the preeminence of the short game. He must learn to relish getting the ball into the hole, to love it as much or more than mere ball-striking.

This is not a truth that I discovered. Good players have known it for generations. Still, lots of people persist in thinking that the key to improvement is learning to hit tee shots like John Daly's. Nothing could be further from the truth. In fact, the closer a golfer gets to hitting as long as John Daly, the more critical his short game becomes.

Early in 1994, I began to work with Daly. We sat down together and talked for five or six hours.

He told me about his drinking problems, his marital problems, his suspension from the Tour. He told me that he often found himself out on the golf course, thinking not about his game, but about all of his personal problems. He told me that hitting the ball as far as he does put even more pressure on him. If he didn't make birdies, he felt he was wasting his potential. That made him angry at himself. Growing up, he had never learned to deal with anger or any other difficult emotion, except by getting drunk.

I taught John the same philosophy and psychology I teach all of my players. While much of what had happened to him in the past was unfortunate, the only question in front of him now was what the rest of the John Daly story would be. He had, I said, the chance to write his own biography. He could be a hero, overcoming great barriers to success, or he could script a sad ending to his golfing career. But it would be his choice. It is a choice he will struggle with for a long time.

As to golf, I told him to work on his game from 120 yards and in.

In addition to his prodigious length, John has fine touch on the greens—he wouldn't have won the PGA at Crooked Stick in 1991 if he hadn't been sinking a lot of putts from five to fifteen feet out. And he has a natural, loose little flop shot from just off the green.

But he will not win much on the Tour without being excellent from 120 yards and in. These are the shots that will create birdies for him. With John's length, he can hit wedges to the green on most par fours. His success will depend, in large part, on whether he can consistently get the ball close enough to the pin from 120 yards and in to make birdies.

Truth be told, though, I tell the same thing to nearly all the players I work with.

A little while ago, I was talking to another strong young pro at the Players Championship. He had just shot a 73, and he was telling me how long he hit the ball and how much potential everyone tells him he has.

I told him that I didn't look at length off the tee when I assessed potential. I want to know how strong a player's mind is, and how well he plays the scoring game with his wedges and his putter.

To explain what I meant, I had him review his round, stroke by stroke, while I made notes. When he was finished, I added up the totals. Of his 73 strokes, 64 fell into just three categories: drives, wedges and putts. Throw out the 14 drives, and he had played 50 strokes with the wedges or the putter.

Then I asked him how much time he thought he ought to be spending on his 3-iron and how much time he ought to be spending on his short game.

The same thing is true, and even more so, with amateurs, from tournament players down to high handicappers. Their short games may not set up as many birdies as John Daly's can. But a weekend player's short game can save pars and turn double-bogeys into bogeys. A solid short game can turn a hacker who can't hit more than a weak banana ball off the tee into a player who shoots in the low 80s or high 70s.

Someday, I am going to talk Tom Kite into conducting an experiment to prove this. We occasionally do clinics together. As I imagine it, at some clinic, he and I will select someone with a handicap of 20 or so to play a round with Tom. The duffer and Tom will each hit the first three shots on par fives, the first two shots on par fours, and the tee shot on par threes. Then they will switch balls. The duffer will hole out Tom's, and Tom will hole out the duffer's.

I am prepared to bet that the score of the ball Tom takes over from the duffer will be lower than the score of the ball the duffer takes over from Tom.

Look at it another way. Nick Price in 1993 led the Tour in scoring average with just under 69 strokes per round. He hit an average of twelve or thirteen greens per round. Most 20-handicappers I see hit at least four or five greens per round. If they had Nick Price's short game, they'd be shooting in the seventies instead of the nineties. But they botch too many shots from 120 yards and in.

Nick tells me that improving his short game has contributed enormously to the improvement in his general attitude over the past few years. He is so confident in his wedges and his putter that he knows he will score well even on days when he's not swinging well. This gives him peace of mind and helps him maintain the mind-set that has characterized his recent play. He can be patient and trusting.

Good short shots are extremely productive. On the average par four, you can hit an excellent drive, a pretty good approach, and still have lots of work left to make par. Foul up one of the putts and you're looking at a bogey. Conversely, you can hit two bad shots with the longer clubs—say, a drive into the rough and a fat approach—and still save your par with an excellent chip or pitch that stops next to the hole. In terms of scoring, the payoff for a good short shot is much higher than the payoff for a good long shot.

Curtis Strange won the U.S. Open in 1989 even though he hit the ball into nine greenside bunkers in the final round. He got up and down eight times. And yet, he appeared in golf magazines thereafter as an exemplar of the swing. His swing didn't win the Open; if he had had a great swing working, he wouldn't have been in nine bunkers. It was his ability to play sand shots, putt, think and stay patient.

A couple of years ago, John Cook, Brad Faxon and Fred Couples were all in the top eight on the money list, but they were all way down in the rankings on driving accuracy. They won money because they all had great short games.

Pat Bradley, during the years she dominated the LPGA Tour, told me that, in her mind, missing a green didn't matter. She was just as intent on, and confident about, holing chips and pitches as she was on long putts. That's how solid her short game was.

Most amateurs have heard about the importance of the short game. But judging by their actions, most don't believe it. At almost any club I visit, I will find ten players standing on the practice tee, whaling away with woods and long irons, for every one I see at a practice green, refining the touch and the shots that will help him or her score.

There's no small amount of *machismo* involved in this. The long drive connotes strength, power, virility. The short game has connotations of delicacy and femininity. Part of my job as a sports psychologist is to help players get past this.

All I can say is that if you want to score well, attach your ego to how well you think, how well you manage your game, how well you hit your wedges, how well you putt. The long-drive swing won't be in the slot every day. But you can always think well, manage your game well, and play the short game well.

The short game is what a lot of great golfers learn first. Bobby Jones spent countless hours on long summer afternoons and evenings chipping and pitching shots to the 13th green at the Atlanta Athletic Club, then sinking the putts.

"I don't remember any glimmering thought of form or any consciousness of a method in playing a shot," Jones wrote later of those boyhood years. "I seemed merely to hit the ball, which is possibly the best way of playing golf."

Sixty years later, in Spain, Jose-Maria Olazabal had much the same kind of early training. He lived on a golf course where his father was the superintendent, and he spent hours and hours chipping and pitching. In the decades between Jones and Olazabal, dozens of great players learned the game by learning the short game first. Some were caddies, pitching and chipping for penny wagers. Tom Kite's father built a bunker and green in his backyard in which Tom spent countless hours. So did the fathers of Ernie Els and Phil Mickelson.

In fact, I would say that most great players first became good at getting the ball into the hole, at the short game. Then, later, they refined their full swings.

Some modern players had the good fortune to have teachers who understood how to inculcate a short game. Tom Kite has told me about how he and Ben Crenshaw learned from Harvey Penick. Tom or Ben would say, for instance, "Mr. Penick, how do you hit a high lob over a trap and stop it real fast?"

Harvey Penick was smart enough not to fill their heads with a lot of instruction about weakening their grips and not turning their right hands over. He gave them some balls and sent them out to a practice green. He told them to stand behind the bunker and pretend there was a tree growing in it. Then they were to hit balls over the tree. They were to make the tree grow higher until it was the right size to make the ball sit down and stop near the hole. And when they could do that, they were to come and tell him about it.

Eventually, Tom and Ben would come running into the pro shop, proudly announcing that they had completed their assignment. Harvey Penick would go out to the practice green and watch.

And if one of them asked him a question about technique for the high lob, Mr. Penick would reply, "I don't know. Show me again." After they'd demonstrated again, he would say, "It's what you just did."

For the short game, he knew that touch, feel and confidence were paramount. And he knew how to teach them.

How do you develop a good short game if you didn't grow up on a golf course, have a backyard bunker, or have Harvey Penick for a teacher?

First of all, you practice it. The professionals that I work with all do. If you're not spending 70 percent of your practice time on shots from 120 yards in, you're not trying to become the best golfer you can be.

The pros play little games in the practice area. They'll have their caddies take a couple of shag bags and put them ten yards apart, a hundred yards out. Then they'll put a towel midway between the bags. Then they'll shoot at the towel. They get a point for every ball that lands between the bags and three for every one that hits the towel. They lose two points for every ball that lands outside the bags. They frequently change the distance they're hitting, of course. Or they play little up and down games around the practice green, frequently for small bets. A player can't get enough of this kind of practice.

Tom Kite has a couple of excellent short-game practice routines.

In the first, he sends his caddie, Mike Carrick, precisely 40 yards out from the practice tee. Tom then tries to hit to a ball bag at Carrick's feet. As soon as he makes contact with the ball Tom yells out the distance he thinks it will go. He might, for instance, yell, "thirty-eight," if he thinks it will land two yards short of Carrick. When the ball lands, Carrick tells him the exact distance it traveled. If it goes precisely to the target, Carrick simply raises his arms over his head—touchdown.

Once he's handling 40 yards, Tom changes to 50, then 60, then 70, and on up to 120. When he's done that, he starts staggering the distances—first 40, then 80, then 60, then 110. In this way, he sharpens his touch with his wedges.

Tom and I often play a similar game from the practice bunker. I'll stand on the green, 20 yards away, and hold out my hand. Tom has to blast the ball close enough to my hand so that I can catch the ball without moving my feet. When he's done that, I move a few steps closer. And then closer, until, in the final stage, I am squatting on the lip of the bunker, just a few yards from Tom, and he has to feather the ball to me the way he would if he were blasting to a tight pin.

I don't suggest that high handicappers try this with their first-born children as catchers, at least not at first. I offer it as an illustration of how well a player like Kite hits wedges, and how hard he works to maintain his touch with the short clubs.

The ideal way to develop a good mental approach to golf would be to learn how to think your way around the green, and then let those skills transfer to the long game. From a psychological point of view, the short game requires the same uncluttered mind, the same focus on the target, and the same disciplined routine that the long game requires—only more so.

What do I mean by more so?

First of all, have no swing thoughts whatsoever from 120 yards and in. Think only of the target.

You will use your standard routine for the short game, except that you may want to make a few more practice swings, eyes focused on your target, until the swing feels right and you can trust it completely.

More so than in the long game, you will have shots that require some adjustments in grip and stance. You may have odd lies. Take care of those adjustments with the first couple of practice swings.

Don't hit the shot thinking about making a weight shift, or how far your backswing should go. That kind of thought introduces tension into the body, and tension can ruin a pitch or chip.

Frequently, the pitch shot you face will be shorter than the distance you get from a full swing with your wedge. This poses a problem for many amateurs. One way to combat it is to know what your optimal wedge distance is and lay up to that distance. If you're 260 yards from the green and you can only hit the ball 230 with your fairway wood, it makes no sense to hit that wood if your favorite approach shot is a wedge from 100 yards. Hit a 6 or a 7-iron, then hit the wedge.

But when you do face a wedge from other than your optimal distance, trust your feel. If you've practiced enough, you'll have it. And don't try to get too cute. If your normal swing produces a 100-yard wedge shot, and your distance is 98 yards, don't start thinking about taking two percent off your normal swing. Even professionals can mess themselves up trying to take just a little off their full swings.

Once you've set up, taken your practice swings, and envisioned the shot, don't freeze over the ball. Look at the target. Swing.

For my professional players, 120 yards from the pin is a threshold distance. From within that range, I want them to be thinking about sinking the shot. The hole is their ultimate target. Obviously, this may be asking a little too much of most amateurs. I would not recommend that a 20-handicapper try to hole a 110-yard wedge shot if the flag is tucked on the far edge of the green, close to a pond—because, by definition, 20-handicappers don't hit their wedges that accurately. Facing such a tight and dangerous pin placement from 110 yards, the 20-handicapper should pick a safer target, closer to the middle of the green. The threshold distance for an amateur might be 40, 60, or 80 yards, depending on his or her skills. Every player has to judge that individually. But inside your threshold distance, don't just go for the middle of the green and don't just try to get it close.

✓ *From inside your threshold distance, think about holing the shot.*

You have to consider how the ball is going to roll once it hits the ground. If the slope of the green is going to make the ball break, you must shift your target accordingly. It may become an imaginary hole two feet to the left of the real hole or five feet right. But whenever possible, you should have your imaginary target be the same distance from the ball as the real target, the hole.

Ninety percent of the players I work with pick a target at the distance they want the ball to travel. This is the way I would teach a youngster to do it. But some players have been brought up to chip or pitch to a landing spot and to think of that as their target. If they have, I don't insist that they change, but I do insist that they commit themselves to spot-chipping every time the same way. The main thing is that the player be thinking about chipping the ball in the hole, not just getting it on the green or getting it close.

There may be occasions when you can't see the hole on a short shot. You might, for instance, be at the bottom of a slope, pitching up to an elevated green. In that situation, think about dropping the ball straight onto the flagstick. This frightens some people. They think the ball will go too long. But the slope of the land causes the ball to pop up higher and land shorter than they expect.

WHEN I FIRST started to work with Davis Love III, he was a student at the University of North Carolina. His father was an old friend of mine from *Golf Digest* schools, and he sent Davis to me for help with the mental side of his game.

As a college student, Davis already had a long, fluid swing and enormous distance. He knew how to hit the short shots, having been taught by his father, who was a master. But his short game wasn't as productive as it would need to be if he wanted to be a successful professional.

I suggested that he approach pitches and chips the way his friend Michael Jordan approached scoring in basketball. Jordan just looked at the basket and shot. I wanted Davis to do the same thing with chips and putts—just look and react. I told him to think of his short game as a run-and-shoot offense.

I threw another metaphor at him, suggesting that it was a lot like playing jazz on the piano. Anyone can learn to put his fingers on the right keys, just as anyone can mechanically place his putter or his wedge in the right spot. But to make beautiful music, a piano player has to let it flow, the way a putter or chipper has to look and react.

Davis also needed to learn to think about holing his short shots. When he first came to me, he was not thinking about getting his chips and pitches into the hole. He was thinking about getting up and down. Sometimes he'd be confident he would. Sometimes he'd be worried he wouldn't. But he was not thinking about the hole.

That had to change before he could win consistently, and it did.

Davis has gotten better every year, and he's become a fine player with his wedge and putter. Of course, I'm particularly happy for him when he wins a tournament with his short game.

A few years ago, at the Tournament of Champions, in the last two rounds, Davis hit something like six fairways and five or six greens. He won the tournament because he had his wedge and putter going so well.

I remember his triumph at the Tournament Players Championship and in particular the way he played the 8th hole at that tournament, a long par three. During the final round, Davis pushed his tee shot a bit and wound up right of the green. He was getting ready to play his second shot when he heard a couple of guys in the gallery behind him making bets about whether he could get up and down. Davis stopped.

He turned toward the bettors and said, "Guys, I'm going to make this shot."

Then he turned around, went through his routine, and holed the pitch for a birdie.

Of course, thinking about the hole doesn't always work quite that well. A few years ago, Brad Faxon got into a sudden-death playoff at the Buick Open. He hit an errant approach and left himself with a nearly impossible shot—from a thin lie, over a bunker to a tight pin. He had to make it to stay alive.

Most players, faced with that shot on national television, would have thought about avoiding disaster. They would have played not to stub it, not to leave the ball in the bunker. They would have been satisfied just getting the ball somewhere on the green.

Not Brad. He took a long, fluid swing and flopped the ball just over the lip of the trap. It trickled down, rolled just over the edge of the cup—and past. Brad fell to the ground, unable to believe it hadn't gone in.

Those are the breaks of the game. The important thing is that Brad had focused sharply on hitting the ball into the hole. If you do that, your misses will be closer and the breaks will, eventually, even out.

Above all in the short game, be decisive. Your model might be Tom Watson's famous chip shot from the deep fringe at the 17th hole at Pebble Beach, the shot that won the U.S. Open in 1982. Bill Rogers, Watson's playing partner, must have taken ten minutes to get the ball from the fringe up to the pin. Watson's mind remained quiet. He took a look at the lie, then returned to stand with his caddie, Bruce Edwards, to wait until it was his turn to play. Then he walked behind the ball, took two practice strokes, decided it felt good, took a last look at the target, and let the shot go.

Most golfers would have hunched over that ball forever, until whatever touch they had was gone. They would have decided that it was good enough just to keep the ball close. Then they would have jabbed at it and sent it skittering past the hole.

But Watson told his caddie he was going to put the ball in the hole. And he did.

10.

What I Learned from Bobby Locke

....
....
....

WHEN I WAS a boy in Rutland, Vermont, I quite accidentally got to know Bobby Locke, the man widely acclaimed as the greatest putter who ever lived. I had a summer job toting clubs at the Rutland Country Club. Locke, coincidentally, had married a Vermont woman, and he spent a few weeks every summer with her family. The Rutland Country Club was the best course around, and he would come by to play a few rounds or give an exhibition. I got his bag.

Altogether unwittingly, from both his perspective and my own, he began my education in that part of golf which is played between the ears.

Bobby Locke did not, to my eyes anyway, look like much of an athlete. He was pear-shaped, with a thin little mustache, and he still wore plus fours and a long-sleeved shirt with a tie, even though this was around 1960.

Nor did he display the fierce demeanor that I had been led to believe was common to all successful athletes. He was not one to get up at dawn. Most days, he would show up at the course around ten in the morning. He'd hit fifteen or twenty wedges, chip and putt for a few minutes, and then go play. He walked very slowly, so much so that some members grumbled when he was on the course. But I noticed that he never spent very much time over the ball.

After his round, he'd spend a few hours in the bar, drinking something like Pabst Blue Ribbon and telling stories.

Years later, when I read his autobiography, I learned that someone had told him early on in his career that a good player had to be relaxed. Locke said he had set out to cultivate relaxation in everything he did. That certainly described the man I knew in Vermont.

It was not that he did not care about how he played, because he did. When he gave an exhibition, he warmed up more thoroughly. The club had no practice range, so he would take some balls to the first tee. I shagged for him, and I brought my baseball glove with me. He started off hitting high 7-irons with a pronounced draw. I would wait until the last moment, break to my right, and make a running catch off the first or second bounce—looking, I no doubt thought, very much like the Red Sox centerfielder of the future.

"Master Bob!" he called out after I had caught a couple. No one had ever called me "Master" before, but it seemed to go with the way he was dressed, so I came running in.

"Master Bob," he said when I arrived. "My ball always will curve to your right. And I want you to walk, leaving early, to catch it. That makes me look good, and this is my show, Master Bob, not yours."

I went back out and shagged balls his way.

At the close of every exhibition, Locke would answer questions. Whenever someone asked him about his putting secret, he would say:

"Well, you just hit it and listen."

And someone would inevitably say, "What do you mean, hit it and listen?"

And Locke would reply, "You just hit it and listen."

Then some genius would ask, "Yeah, but don't you want to see if you make it?"

And Locke would respond, "I don't have to see if I make it. I can hear it."

Then some real genius would pipe up, "Well, if you miss it, don't you want to see how it will break coming back?"

And Locke would say, "Why would I want to see it if I miss it?"

The point, I now realize, was that he wanted nothing to impair his confidence.

He didn't want to dwell on the putts that he missed, because that would only make it harder to be certain that the next one was going in. And that was one thing Locke insisted upon. Putting was about confidence. "Hitting a putt in doubt is fatal in most cases," he wrote in his autobiography. Locke had to be certain that the putt was going in. Looking back, I can believe that he was.

PHYSICALLY, PUTTING IS the simplest of all the golf strokes. Anyone who can toss a beanbag underhanded into a wastebasket has the required coordination.

The style of the stroke is unimportant. There have been great wrist putters and great shoulder putters. There are good putters who putt cross-handed. Johnny Miller won the AT&T Pro-Am at

Pebble Beach in 1994 with something he called the claw grip. Bernhard Langer won the Masters in 1993 putting with one hand clasped to his forearm.

Yet, you can still find teachers who will dissect the "proper" stroke and grip at great length and insist that their pupils master these mechanics.

I don't think there is a classic putting stroke. Locke took the putter back a little to the inside of the target line, with a closed stance and a slightly hooded clubface, to put overspin on the ball. All of those things were wrong, if you go by the conventional wisdom about putting mechanics.

Brad Faxon told me a story about a friend of his who is a teaching pro and Ben Crenshaw. The teacher called Faxon and asked for help in getting inside the ropes at a tournament practice green, so that he could videotape Crenshaw's putting stroke. Faxon agreed.

Crenshaw, as usual, was friendly and accommodating as the teacher taped his practice putts. The teacher got more comfortable.

"Ben, will you tell me what you're working on while I have the tape running?" he asked.

Crenshaw obliged.

"I'm trying to make sure my head and my knees move a little and my stroke feels longer," he said. "Because when it feels like that, I always putt real well. But every once in a while, you start getting a little careful, and you try to make sure your head stays still. And if your head stays too still, you lose your feel and you start putting badly. You can never putt well without feel."

The teacher was dumbfounded. The best putter in the world had just denied one of the tenets he held sacred about the mechanics of putting, the still head.

The point is not that the head should move and the stroke

should be long. Or that the head should be still and the stroke short. The point is that what's important is not the mechanics of Crenshaw's stroke, but his feel for it, his belief in it, his trust that it will make the ball go in the hole. When doubts started to erode this confidence, he had to catch himself and get back that feeling of trust.

Attitude is what makes a great putter.

Putting is largely mental, and you have control over your mind and attitude. To become a good putter, you must make a commitment to good thinking. You have to fill your mind with thoughts that will help you, not excuses for poor putting. You have to decide that, come what may, you love putting and you're glad that every hole gives you a chance to use your putter, because that's where you've got a big advantage over all the players who dread putting.

Nick Price, when he was dominating the tour in the summer of 1994, told me he was so confident when he stepped up to a straight putt he almost felt as if he were cheating. That kind of confidence guaranteed that he would make a lot of putts.

The late Davis Love, Jr., once told me an illustrative story about putting attitude. Love had himself been a touring pro, and for a while in the 1950s he cut expenses by sharing a motel room with another young pro, Gary Player.

Their first tournament together was on a course down South with very slow Bermuda greens. This occurred before the development of the modern, hybrid Bermudas, and the greens on this course were like shag rugs. Love thought they were the worst he'd ever played on. But every night, Player would come back to the room and talk about how much he loved slow, shaggy Bermuda greens.

The next week, they drove north to a course with bent-grass greens, which the superintendent had shaved until they were like linoleum. Player, of course, came back to the room talking about how much he loved to play fast, bent-grass greens, the faster the better. Love couldn't stand the contradiction.

"Which is it, Gary? Do you love slow, Bermuda greens" he asked, "or fast, bent greens?"

"You just have to love whatever greens you're playing on," Player replied.

To someone unfamiliar with the way great athletes think, Player's attitude would seem to verge on foolishness. A golfer might like fast greens or slow greens or medium greens, but he cannot rationally like fast greens one week and slow greens the next. And only a fool could stand over a twenty-foot putt and be absolutely confident of holing it, when he has a lifetime of experience to prove that his chances of doing so are really about one in ten.

But this kind of foolishness is precisely what all great putters have in common.

Losing that foolishness is what happens to players when they get what are commonly called the yips.

There is no neurological basis for the yips. Nothing about the physical aging process dictates that a golfer cannot putt as well at sixty as he did at twenty.

The great players usually start out as confident putters, even bold putters. But over the years, even the great ones have trouble maintaining this attitude. Maybe playing for years with major championships on the line inevitably produces memories of missed putts in crucial situations. After a while, those memories become so burdensome that the golfer can't keep them out of his mind as he stands on the green. Then he loses the instinct to look at the hole, look at the ball, let the putt go, and know that it's going in.

In other cases, a player's ball-striking actually improves as he gets older. Then it becomes agonizingly apparent that the only thing that is keeping him from winning is his putting, particularly his short putts. That places enormous pressure on his putting, pressure that did not exist when he was younger and could blame other flaws in his game for his bad rounds. Little doubts and smidgens of indecision creep into his mind as he putts.

Then, perhaps, the problem becomes public knowledge. People hear that Hogan can't putt anymore, or Snead can't putt anymore, or Watson can't putt anymore. Golf magazines write about it. Johnny Miller talks about it. That multiplies the pressure. Pretty soon, the only thing the golfer can think about when he stands over an important four-footer is, "The whole world knows I can't make this kind of putt anymore."

At this point, fear infects the player's mind, and fear destroys putting. A good putting attitude is free of fear. A good putting attitude blends ideas that almost seem contradictory. The golfer has to believe the putt will go in the hole, but he must not care if he misses. He has to try enough to maintain a disciplined routine focused on sinking the putt, but not try so hard that he tightens up. He has to find a balance between determination and nonchalance.

Arnold Palmer, in his prime, instinctively had that balanced attitude toward putting. A few years ago, he and I were speaking at a corporate golf outing in New York. I was talking to the duffers in the audience, or so I thought, when I made some comments about nerves and putting. I told them that golfers don't physically lose their nerve on the greens. They simply start buying the myth that age brings on the yips. Then they lose the habit of looking at the hole and reacting to it with confidence.

"That's exactly my problem!"

It was Palmer, breaking in, unable to contain himself. "That's what I'm doing!"

Palmer went on for ten minutes. In his youth, he said, he had been decisive, even bold on the greens. But he wasn't any longer. He had become careful and tentative. He had to get back to being decisive.

I respected him enormously for speaking publicly about it. Upon reflection, I was not surprised that he did. Playing golf well demands honesty. Palmer would not have become great if he had been in the habit of deluding himself. I think that this willingness to confront the problems in his mental game and not to blame them on the inevitable onslaught of the yips is one reason he will keep winning the occasional Skins Game to supplement his Social Security checks.

Unlike Palmer, most players have their putting confidence spoiled well before they become champions. There is a process of socialization at work. As kids of twelve or thirteen, I think most golfers, if they have any athletic talent, are instinctively good putters. Like the young Bobby Jones, the good natural putter begins by simply walking up to the ball and rapping it at the hole.

But eventually, the good young putter will miss a five-footer. And when he does, some well-meaning adult will tell him that he missed it because he was too casual. He will tell him that putting is hard. He will tell him to size up every five-foot putt as if he were buying the putting surface instead of playing on it. And the youngster will start to tighten up and get careful with his putts, the way the 20-handicappers at the club do. More often than not, he'll be on his way to having a 20 handicap himself.

But kids, before their attitudes are spoiled, have a confident approach to putts. A few years ago, I was watching the Buick Open. Brad Faxon had a six-footer to win the tournament. My daughter, Casey, who was about nine years old, walked into the room and noticed that the adults were all nervous. She asked why, and I explained the situation.

"Oh, that's nothing," she said, mystified by our attitudes. "Brad always makes those." She left the room, supremely confident in Brad. And Brad made it.

Brad doesn't always make them, but any golfer will make more putts if he can get close to Casey's attitude.

I remember once watching, along with Tom Kite's mother, as Ben Crenshaw sank a few long putts to win a tournament.

"That's nothing compared to the way he used to putt," Mrs. Kite said. "When Ben was a boy, he'd just walk up to the ball and hit it. He generally didn't even bother to squat down behind it and read the green. And he sank putts from all over."

Over the years, Ben has gotten more deliberate and careful. And though he's still very relaxed on the green compared with most golfers, and he's still a wonderful putter, I'd love to know whether he's any better now than he was when he was a teenager.

WHEN TOURING PROS come to me for help with their putting, we begin as we begin for all shots, by establishing a good routine. All routines have personal variations, of course, and the putting routine differs somewhat from the full-swing and short-game routines because it has to allow for reading the green.

You might, as you read the putt, want to walk around the cup if this helps you see the whole putt. But I don't like to see golfers pace off the distance between the ball and the hole. This promotes an analytical, mechanical approach to something that must be based on feel. If you plumb-bob, which some touring pros do, insert it into your routine at this stage.

The important thing is that you commit yourself completely to the read you make. A decisive attitude is much more important in putting than reading the minute breaks and the grain of the grass.

It's easy to fall into the trap of overreading a putt. Frequently I find that players would do better if they didn't bother trying to read putts at all, if they walked onto the green, looked quickly at the line, and hit the ball.

Blaine McAllister did just that a short time ago in the B.C. Open. He came to the final green brimming with confidence, tied for the lead in the tournament. He had an eight-footer left. He was so confident that he didn't bother to line it up. He just walked up to it and hit it in the hole, for the win.

When we talked on the phone afterward, Blaine was still overjoyed by the confidence he'd displayed. I told him it was a good thing he'd let that confidence dictate his putting. A lot of players would have analyzed that eight-footer until it looked like a freeway interchange. They would have found it impossible to believe that such an important putt could be straight; they'd have read the green until they found a break. Then they would get tentative and leave the ball either short or long. They'd have left themselves a three-footer to tie and gotten even more nervous. It happens all the time. People who overread are, as Billy Casper once said, often really looking for a way to miss rather than a way to make the putt. And they forget a most important principle:

It's more important to be decisive about a read than correct.

ONCE YOU'VE MADE a decisive read, you need to think about, or visualize, the line of the putt. As with full shots, this step depends on individual idiosyncrasies. Some golfers can envision the line of the putt as clearly as they can see a yellow line painted down the middle of a highway. Others don't see anything in their mind's eye. But they nevertheless convince themselves that the line is right and the putt will drop. That's all that's important.

Next, for most players, it's time to pick out a target. There are no intermediate targets in putting, because an intermediate target might confuse you about how hard to hit it. For a straight putt, obviously, you use the cup for your target, but not the whole cup. Pick a particular spot in the cup.

For breaking putts, you will have to improvise a target. The idea is to try to make all putts seem straight. If you think the putt will break two feet to the right, pick out something two feet to the left of the hole—a spike mark, a discolored blade of grass, or a grain of sand. This can be difficult on courses with excellent, uniform greens, and you may have to settle for a spot in the grass. Or, you can just imagine a hole at the end of the line on which your putt will start.

On uphill and downhill putts, your imaginary target may be a foot or two in front of or behind the hole. Occasionally it will be even further than that. There are greens with humps and ridges, and the right target may be a spot at the crest of a ridge, from which gravity will pull the ball down to the hole.

Once you have selected your target, focus on it exclusively. Don't let your eyes wander to the cup.

There can be individual variations. Brad Faxon concentrates on the entire path of the putt, rather than an imaginary hole-high target, from the time he reads the putt until the time he strikes the ball.

Speed is a critical factor, especially on slick greens, but I don't advise players to think too much about it. The best putters don't.

Faxon, who consistently ranks near the top of the PGA putting statistics, tells me he never thinks about speed. He goes entirely by instinct, an instinct honed, of course, by a lot of practice and playing experience.

There is a way of thinking that can help you get the speed right. For a downhill putt, tell yourself that you want the ball to barely make it over the front lip of the cup on its last rotation. For an uphill putt, you might think of hitting the ball so it strikes the back of the cup as it goes down.

As far as speed is concerned, I have no quarrel with players who try to make their putts die in the hole. Many of the greatest players in the game did that. Other players believe in putting firmly, so the ball bounces off the back of the cup, particularly on short putts. I don't care which method a putter chooses, as long as he's focused on putting the ball in the hole.

If you miss short very often, it may be a sign of tentativeness and indecision. People who leave it short due to fear are afraid of running it too far past the hole and missing the return putt. If that's why someone is leaving putts short, it's a problem to be corrected.

But remember that the goal is neither to hit them firm nor to have them die at the hole, but to sink them. Don't be distracted from this objective by concerns about missing short or missing close.

A few years ago, the basketball coach at James Madison University, Lou Campanelli, called me. He asked if I could help one of his players, a senior who had previously been a good free-throw shooter. In his final season, Lou said, this kid was breaking the backboard with every free throw he attempted. He was still a fine field-goal shooter, but his free-throw percentage was way down. Every shot he took was long.

I went to talk to the young man and asked him when his free-throw problem started.

"I don't know," he said. "The first game of the year, I guess."

Anything prior to that, I prodded.

"Well, in the NCAA tournament last year," he said, "we were playing North Carolina and we had a chance to upset them. Inside the last minute, it was a one-point game. I went to the free-throw line with a one-and-one. And I shot an airball. They brought it inbounds, but after about ten seconds we stole it. I had the ball and the whole North Carolina team attacked me. I thought, my gosh, they want me on the line.

"I thought I was composed, but as soon as I was set to shoot, the North Carolina fans started chanting: 'Airball.' That really got to me, and I barely ticked the rim with my shot. North Carolina went on to win the game.

"I had let myself down and I had let my teammates down. Before I left the locker room, I made a commitment to myself that I would never shoot an airball again."

"Congratulations," I said. "Keep on doing what you're doing and you'll never shoot another airball. But if you want to make free throws, you have to change your thinking. You have a perfect attitude for avoiding airballs, but a lousy attitude for making free throws. If you want to be a great free-throw shooter, you have to accept an airball now and then."

Golfers can do the analogous thing. In their eagerness to stop leaving their putts short (and being called "Alice") or to stop running them too far past, they can lose focus on the real goal, which is putting the ball into the cup. The putter who is called Alice on the first green runs putts five or ten feet past on the next seventeen holes. Or the putter who runs one way past on the first green becomes tentative. What they don't do is knock anything difficult into the hole.

So, YOU'VE READ the green decisively and picked out a line or a target. You may at this point in your routine want to take a couple of practice strokes. Take them with your eyes on the target, not the ball, and certainly not on the putter blade. Use them to make sure you feel the right stroke for the distance the ball has to travel. If you look at the ball or the blade, it will only introduce questions into your mind about the path the blade is taking, mechanical questions that divert you from your focus on the target.

The next step is getting yourself aligned and aimed properly. Many of the players I work with use the lettering on their golf balls to aid in doing this. They mark their balls, clean them, and then replace them so that the lettering is precisely in line with the intended line of the putt. Then they take their stances and use the lettering to align the blade of the putter.

Though there's no particular stance or grip that makes for good putting, there is one mechanical point worth mentioning in the alignment process. The eyes see the putt better when they are precisely over the ball. As a golfer develops a putting routine, it's worth practicing this indoors. Put a mirror on the floor and place the ball on it. Adjust your stance until your eyes are right over the ball or just inside it, whichever works better for you.

Once you've aimed yourself, you have to trust that your routine works and you're aimed correctly. Sometimes, a green will have undulations placed purposely by the architect to create optical illusions and confuse players. Don't let them distract you. Be decisive. If you take your stance, look at the target, and start wondering whether you're aimed correctly, you need to walk away and start the process over again, because you can't putt decisively if you're questioning your aim. Don't worry about slowing play down. If you are this meticulous about trusting your routine, you will make up for the lost time in the long run by taking fewer putts.

The heart of the putting routine is analogous to the core of the exemplary routines for full shots and the short game: *Look at the target. Look at the ball. Let the putt go.*

Two principles, by now familiar to you, underlie this postulate. One is that your brain and nervous system work best when the brain simply reacts to the target. The other is that the longer a player stands over the ball before he hits the putt, the more likely he is to allow the intrusion of mechanical thoughts or doubts that will corrupt the pure, simple interplay among the target, the brain, and the nervous system.

The "run-and-shoot" attitude that Davis Love III borrowed for his short game from watching Michael Jordan play basketball exemplifies this. The idea is to let the conscious mind step aside and let the subconscious react to the target. Think when you're behind the ball. Don't think when you're over it. Do.

As with the full swing, there is a rhythm to looking at the target, looking at the ball, and letting the putt go. When I begin to work with a player, we spend a lot of time getting this rhythm ingrained in his or her routine. The player strokes one five-footer after another in time with my voice: Look at the target. Short pause. Look at the ball. Short pause. Let it go. It's almost like a mantra.

If a player I've been working with develops putting problems and asks me for help, the first thing I check is his rhythm. Is he following his routine in competition at the same pace he did on the practice green? If he's not, particularly if the pause between looking at the ball and letting the putt go has lengthened, that's a sign that he's not getting himself into a decisive frame of mind before he strokes the putt.

This is especially important on short putts. In every round, a golfer will have some critical putts of three to six feet. And everyone I work with, from high handicappers to the winners of major championships, occasionally has trouble with them.

Short putts remind me of field-goal kicks in football. Kicking field goals has little in common with the elements of football that most coaches like to emphasize: blocking, tackling, running. It's a simple task that comes down not so much to strength as to trust. But so many games are decided by field goals that no sensible coach would send a team onto the field without a good kicker. Similarly, no golfer should approach competition without a confident attitude toward short putts.

You have to begin by committing yourself to liking them. You will not be one of the guys who sit in the locker room complaining about what great scores they'd be shooting if they weren't blowing short putts. You will, instead, be a player who loves holing short putts. You will roll them just as freely as you roll 40-foot putts. You won't try to steer them or overcontrol them.

You can do this, in part, by practicing them. As you practice, emphasize being trusting and decisive with each putt. In most cases, this will mean hitting it firmly. I advise my professionals to do this with all short putts, taking some of the break out of them.

You won't, of course, make all your short putts. But when, inevitably, you miss a short putt, ask yourself why you missed it. Did you misread the green, or get the speed wrong? If so, forget it. But if you missed it because you were afraid of missing it and got tentative and careful, because you really didn't believe you would make it, redouble your effort to be trusting and decisive. If you do, you will still miss some short putts. But you will be a good short putter. You will miss less often.

On long putts, the biggest fallacy I see players falling for is the three-foot target. This is an imaginary circle with a radius of three feet and the hole at the center. Some teachers suggest a player facing a long putt should try only to get the ball inside this circle. This makes no sense. Think about an archer or a pistol shooter. They shoot at an artificial target with a bull's-eye and concentric outer circles. But no matter what the distance, they always aim for the bull's-eye. It gives them the biggest margin of error. Even if they miss it, they're likely to hit something on the target. The same principle applies to putting. Always aim to make it.

It's not hard to be decisive if the ball is going in the hole for you. Anybody who makes a couple of long putts on the first two holes is going to be decisive when he putts on the third green. The hard part is remaining decisive even if the first critical putts of the day don't fall.

This bedeviled Nick Price and a lot of professionals. I've had players tell me that they actually hope they don't hit their approach shots stiff on the first few holes. This sounds incredible, but the fact is they don't want to risk blowing a few makable birdie putts, because they know from experience that if they miss a couple of short birdie putts on the first few holes, their putting will be tentative and ineffective the rest of the day. Responding positively to missed putts is a major challenge.

The question you must ask yourself is not whether you're sinking your putts. The proper question is whether your attitude is giving your putts a chance to go in. If it is, you should be encouraged by missed putts. Sooner or later, since you're doing everything right, putts will start to fall. The law of averages, if you've just missed a few, suggests it will be sooner rather than later.

But if you have to admit to yourself that you have not been trusting and decisive with your putting, then you have a choice. You can let your missed putts make you even more tentative and indecisive for the rest of the day, and hope that geese land on the green and peck your errant putts into the hole. Or you can decide to become even more decisive and trusting in your putting and give yourself a chance to make some.

I recall Tom Watson at the 1982 U.S. Open. Everyone remembers the chip shot he sank at the 17th hole to seal the win. But equally impressive to me was the way he reacted after missing a straight, two-foot putt on the 7th green. He missed it so badly that it didn't even touch the cup. But he refused to get flustered and refused to get tentative.

On the next hole, he buried an 18-footer for birdie, getting back the lost stroke and a share of the lead with Jack Nicklaus. Some time after that, I asked him what had gone through his mind on those two holes. He told me that his miss only showed that even great putters miss an occasional easy one. He was a great putter. He acknowledged that it was disappointing and unfortunate to miss a two-footer in the final round of the U.S. Open. But he reminded himself that if he wanted to continue to be a great putter, he had to give himself a chance on the next hole and the ones after that.

In candor, Watson said, he knew that giving himself a chance would not guarantee that the next birdie putt would fall. But back in the days when he was putting well, that was what he knew he had to do.

11.

Golf Is Not a Game of Perfect

A FEW YEARS ago, Tom Kite and I were in Austin, and we played a round at Lakeway Country Club with a couple of members of the University of Texas golf team. It was a beautiful day and a great match. They all shot between 69 and 73. Afterward, we all sat down for a soda, and it was obvious they were dying to ask a question. So I said, "What's on your mind?"

One of the guys replied, "Tom, we basically hit it as good as you did today. When we missed and hit a bunker, our bunker shots were as good as yours. When we missed a green, we got it up and down like you did. We scored within a shot or two of one another. So how come you're the all-time leading money winner and we're the number three and four golfers at the University of Texas?"

Tom grinned at me and said, "Do you want to tell them?"

"No," I said. "They'll believe it more if it comes from you."

"The difference," Tom said, "is that when you guys get in tournaments, the likelihood is that you'll lose your concentration on four or five shots every round. Over a four-day tournament, even if every lapse costs you just one stroke, that's sixteen to twenty shots a week, and that's the difference between being the leading money winner and losing your card. If one of these lapses costs you two or three strokes, or you get upset and lose concentration on a second shot, you can be talking about twenty-five to thirty strokes a week, and you won't even make the college golf team. Over a career, losing concentration once in a while can mean lots of strokes."

I joined in. "Today, each of you hit a few balls off line, into the rough or the trees. But since it wasn't a tournament round, you didn't let it bother you. You just went over and found the ball, pitched out, wedged up to the green, saved your par and went on. But in the Southwest Conference Tournament, you might hit the same shot and overreact to it. You start telling yourself, 'You're such a jerk,' and 'Why does this always happen in a big tournament?' Before you even hit your next shot, you're convinced you're going to make bogey or double-bogey. And you do."

One of the things Tom, or any successful pro, does best is to accept his bad shots, shrug them off, and concentrate completely on the next one. He has accepted the fact that, as he puts it, "Golf is not a game of perfect."

This does not mean that a pro doesn't strive to eliminate mistakes from his game. He does, unless he wants to savor the joy of Qualifying School once again. But he understands that while striving for perfection is essential, demanding perfection of himself on the golf course is deadly.

Of all the tournaments Tom Kite has won, one of the most impressive to me was at Bay Hill a few years ago. He and Davis

Love both butchered the final hole. Tom hit his approach in the water and Davis flew his over the green. What impressed me was the way Tom responded to the shot that went in the water. He then had to play a long wedge shot over the same water to a tight pin. He could have dwelled on the way he hit the last shot so badly. He could have tried for the middle of the green or even the bunker, just to make sure he didn't make two splashes in a row. Instead, he hit that second wedge stiff, made the putt, and went on to win the playoff.

The television announcers and the golf writers weren't impressed. They don't think a guy who hits his ball into the water on the last hole deserves to win the golf tournament. But I knew how brilliantly Tom had responded to one of the fundamental challenges of the game:

No matter what happens with any shot you hit, accept it. Acceptance is the last step in a sound routine.

When I next talked to Tom, he had almost bought into the attitude of the writers and commentators that there was something wrong with the way he'd won the tournament. I told him that, on the contrary, there was a great deal to admire in it.

Tom had wanted to win, desperately. He had hit a bad shot. But he hadn't reacted by losing his concentration. Instead, he got up and down and went on to win the tournament.

"You know, Tom," I said, "no matter how good you get at this game, a lot of funky, crazy things are going to happen on the golf course. The better you can get at accepting them, the better you're going to get."

Good golfers, I think, have to get over the notion that they only want to win by hitting perfect shots. They have to learn to enjoy winning ugly. And that entails acceptance of all the shots they hit, not just the good ones.

The next week, as it happened, Tom won the TPC with a

display of nearly perfect golf. The writers and commentators all swooned at his feet. But I still like the win at Bay Hill a little better.

I FIND IT amusing and ironic that players like Tom and Nick Price, who are among the best ball strikers in the world, who practice regularly, can learn to accept their bad shots, while the high-handicappers I see in pro-ams and clinics often cannot. If Price or Kite pushes one into the woods, which he occasionally does, he accepts it as something that is going to happen in golf and he calmly plans his next shot. In fact, the best Tour players make a remarkable number of birdies from out of the woods. They know that escape from the woods demands that they become even calmer and more sharply focused than they normally are.

But the high-handicapper, who's got a loop in his swing the size of the Washington Beltway, who practices twice a year if the weather is good, will fume and curse and berate himself if he hits one into the woods. How could he have been so stupid as to slice the ball?

I've had guys in pro-ams turn to me after a tee shot that wiped out two squirrels and a woodpecker and say, "I don't hit the ball that way."

To which I am tempted to reply, "That's funny, I thought I just saw that you did."

No one likes to hit a bad shot. Let's suppose you're on the first tee at your club in the first round of the club championship and you pull-hook your drive into the trees. This can happen to the best of players. At my home course, Farmington Country Club, at the U.S. Senior Amateur in 1993, the eventual winner hit his very first tee shot out of bounds on the first day of qualifying. Did this make him happy? Of course not.

But the question is, does it do any good to get angry?

Getting angry is one of your options. But if you choose to get angry, you are likely to get tighter. That's going to hurt your rhythm and your flow. It will upset you and distract you. It will switch on your analytical mind and your tendency to criticize and analyze anything you do that falls short of perfection. It will start you thinking about the mechanical flaws in your swing and trying to correct them.

You will very likely play worse.

Alternatively, you could train yourself to accept the fact that as a human being, you are prone to mistakes. Golf is a game played by human beings. Therefore, golf is a game of mistakes.

The best golfers strive to minimize mistakes, but they don't expect to eliminate them. And they understand that it's most important to respond well to the mistakes they inevitably make.

Chip Beck has one of the best attitudes toward bad shots. When he hits it into the woods, he walks toward the ball and all he says is, "You gotta love it. This is what golf is all about."

And he's right. Golf is indeed all about recovering from bad shots. It's about getting up and down from sand traps. It's about knowing when it's smart to pitch sideways out of the rough and do your best to save par or bogey with your wedge and putter. It's about the exhilaration that comes from spotting a narrow path through the trees and threading your ball through it to the green. Viewed this way, any round you play will be enjoyable.

But if you bring a smothering perfectionism to the golf course, you will probably leave with a higher handicap and a lousy disposition, because your game will never meet your expectations.

Some good players have developed idiosyncratic ways of diverting the anger that bubbles up within them after a bad shot.

Sherry Steinhauer tells me that she thinks of her memory as a video machine. If she hits a bad shot during the course of a round, she thinks about erasing the tape of that shot. It's a way of putting the mistake out of her mind. Others think of filing the memory of the mistake away somewhere, or changing the channel on the television.

Jack Nicklaus had a few tricks of his own. Nicklaus nearly always selected his own club and generally wanted only silence and a dry towel from his regular caddie, Angelo Argea. But if he hit a bad shot, he might turn to the innocent Angelo and chew him out, saying, "Damn it, why did you let me pick that thing out of the bag?"

Angelo was smart enough not to take it personally. He knew that Nicklaus would play much better if he directed his anger at his caddie rather than at himself.

Arnold Palmer and Bernhard Langer tend to blame their clubs, frequently switching from one set to another and banishing the offending implements to a dark basement. Langer has been known to soak his clubs in a barrel of water overnight as punishment for their betrayal. He did that the week he won his first Masters.

But if you don't happen to have an understanding caddie in your employ, and you don't have an endorsement contract with a manufacturer who is willing to supply an infinite number of clubs, how do you handle anger?

The first thing to do is to throw away your expectations as soon as you step onto the golf course, and just play. It's very difficult to do. But I have never worked with a golfer who could play anywhere close to his potential unless he shed his expectations before the first shot.

Expectations are great if you confine them to long-range considerations. It's fine, for example, to expect that if you work at your game intelligently for an extended period of time, you will improve. But expectations can hurt you if they are narrowly focused on the results of a particular stroke, hole or round.

Golfers in American society, though, tend to be people who are used to getting what they want. Many were born into families of wealth and achievement. Many of those who were not are people who rose to positions of wealth and status because of ambition and hard work. They expect to master golf just as they've mastered everything else in life. If they are competing, they expect to win. If they swing at a golf ball, they expect to hit it well, every time. When their golf fails to meet their expectations, what happens? They begin to judge how well they are doing against how well they expected to do. They get angry at themselves. They tie themselves up in knots.

This is not to say you should not think about hitting every ball to the target and believe that every shot will do just that. You should. But there is a fine difference between believing that the ball will go where you want it to go and expecting that it will and being upset if it doesn't. You have to put expectations out of your mind by the time you get to the first tee.

On the first tee, you should have two immediate goals. One is to have fun. The other involves the process of playing, not the results. This goal is to get your mind where it's supposed to be on every shot. If you do that, you'll shoot the best score you're capable of shooting that day, whether it's 67 or 107.

Having fun shouldn't be so difficult. You are, after all, out in the fresh air. You are playing in what amounts to an emerald park. Clipped grasslands, according to one theorist, have been the most soothing and emotionally satisfying habitat for man since the first humans dropped out of the trees. You are, presumably, in good company, the company of other golfers. You have a chance to strike a little ball and send it flying straight and true against the sky, an act that seems to resonate pleasantly somewhere deep within the human brain. These are the reasons you initially liked golf even though you couldn't play it very well. Savor all of them as you play. Let the joy of the game come to you.

Shooting the best score you're capable of on a given day requires that, to paraphrase something that's become trite, you become your own best friend—or in this case, a good caddie and pro to yourself. Can you imagine someone paying a caddie to berate him after a bad shot in this fashion: "You left that putt short! You're a wimp! No guts!" Can you imagine someone paying a teaching pro to get apoplectic and tell him he's an idiot for slicing the ball? Or to visit his hotel room after a bad round and remind him of all the mistakes he made that day?

No one would do it. Yet, every time I play golf, I see people doing it to themselves.

You have to be nonjudgmental. You have to forgive and forget and be compassionate toward yourself. But in our culture, people, particularly high achievers, are taught to judge themselves harshly. They're taught that being compassionate toward oneself is weak and indulgent. There is a kernel of truth in this. There is a time and place for tough self-evaluation, and you will not improve as a golfer unless you honestly examine your game and work on its weaknesses.

But don't do it on the golf course.

When a shot is done, it's done. The only constructive thing you can do about it is to hit the next shot as well as you can. That requires that you stay optimistic and enthusiastic.

If you must have expectations about results, expect to make some mistakes. Walter Hagen once said that he expected to make seven mistakes per round. When he hit a bad shot, he wasn't bothered. It was just one of the expected seven.

Acceptance allows a golfer to be patient, and patience is one of the necessary virtues in golf. Sometimes, players tell me they are sick and tired of hearing me say that they must be patient and keep believing that if they do all the right things, the results they want will follow. That's just one more thing they have to learn to be patient about.

If you remember to have fun, it shouldn't be too hard. When was the last time you were impatient when you were having fun?

Remember, too, that golf is not a game of justice. A player can practice properly, think properly, and still hit a bad shot. Or he can hit a good shot and watch a bad hop or a gust of wind deposit the ball in a sand trap.

A golfer can't force results to happen. He can only do everything possible to give those results a chance to happen. As Tom Watson once put it, to become a really good golfer, you have to learn how to wait. But you have to learn to wait with confidence.

ON THE TOUR, there are many factors conspiring to raise a player's expectations, to encourage him to demand perfection of himself. When this happens, the work ethic that brought a lot of players to the Tour can become a double-edged sword, driving an individual to grind himself down in a dogged, joyless attempt to meet those expectations. A successful player has to develop the ability to evaluate himself objectively, to work harder when he needs more practice, but to ease up when he's tempted to push too hard.

Scott Verplank won his first PGA tournament, the Western

Open, while he was still an amateur. He expected that his golf could only get better once he finished school and could commit himself totally to golf, practicing as long as he wanted, playing all the time.

It didn't immediately work out that way for him. Performances that would have won or at least finished in the top ten in any amateur tournament didn't make the cut on the Tour. He perceived them as failures. He responded as most good athletes have been taught to do, by working harder. He practiced all the time. He practiced when he shouldn't have, when what he really needed and wanted to do was sit in his hotel room and read a book. And the hard work didn't show up in better results. Eventually, he found himself returning periodically to Oklahoma State and asking the football coach to let him help out with the running backs. It was the only way he could take his mind off golf.

Talking with him before the Buick Open one year, I emphasized the need for him to take it easy on himself. I told him it would be all right to stay in his room and read a book for a few hours instead of going to the practice tee all day. And I asked him to promise me that he would try to have fun.

I returned to Charlottesville to teach. On Thursday evening, I got a call from Scott.

"Gosh, Doc," he said, "I did it! I had fun all day long. And I'm leading! But what was really great was that I missed a five-footer on the first hole and I didn't let it get to me! Made a thirty-five-footer on the second hole."

"I bet you were invited into the press tent afterward," I said.

"Yeah, I was," he replied.

"And I bet that they asked whether Scott Verplank could win his first tournament as a professional."

"Yeah, that's all they talked about."

"Well, if you're not careful, they're going to have you thinking about the results you get instead of having fun. You might go out there fixed on shooting a certain number and keeping the lead and getting in position to win. You have to remember to throw away expectations, to just have fun and see what's the lowest score you can shoot. You have to attend to the process, not concern yourself with the results."

Of course, I would not be telling this story if it didn't have a happy ending. Scott won the tournament, and he called me up on Sunday evening. After telling me what happened, he said he was being interviewed by the golf writer for a newspaper in Dallas, and he was having trouble explaining to him why the idea of having fun had just helped him win a breakthrough golf tournament. Then he put the writer on.

I talked for a while about the necessity to relax, enjoy the game and accept mistakes if a player wants to do his best. The writer still didn't see it. He couldn't understand why having fun could be difficult.

"Try this," I said. "Tomorrow in your paper, ask everyone in Dallas who plays golf to try a two-week experiment. During the first week, after every shot that's less than perfect, they should get disgusted and angry with themselves. And they should stay mad even after they leave the course and go home. I guarantee you every one of your readers will be able to do it.

"The second week, tell them that after every shot, no matter what happens to it, they are not going to be bothered. They are to have fun, stay decisive, and keep ripping the ball to the target. They are going to have a ball no matter what they shoot.

"You can offer a big cash prize to anyone who can do what you ask during the second week, because I guarantee you there won't be many people, if any, who will be honestly able to collect it."

• • •

RETIREES SOMETIMES HAVE a problem analogous to Scott Verplank's. He expected his golf game to improve immediately once he finished school and could play all the time. Retirees often expect to get good after they stop working and don't have to confine their play to weekends.

When it doesn't happen that way, it's often because they forget that golf remains a game. They practice more, but they also raise their expectations every time they step onto the course. They forget how to laugh off mistakes.

Players plagued by perfectionism and unforgiving expectations would do well to remember the common sense their mothers taught them, or would have taught them if they'd paid attention.

Here's what Adela Saraceni told her son, Gene Sarazen, about perfectionism and expectations, just after he lost the 1927 U.S. Open by a single shot:

"Son, everything that happens to you happens for the best. Don't ever forget that. You can't win all the time, son."

Gene Sarazen said this little bit of advice stuck with him and helped him to develop a certain fatalism about his golf that allowed him to accept whatever happened and make the best of it.

If Mrs. Saraceni were around today, I might be out of business.

12.

Anyone Can Develop
Confidence

I WILL BE revealing no secrets by stating that good golf requires confidence.

Coaches and athletes in all sports have long recognized that teams don't win and athletes don't perform well without confidence.

All of the ideas and techniques I teach to golfers, from free will to the preshot routine, are intended to produce confidence. Without confidence, you can't trust your physical ability. You can't perform at your best.

But a lot of golfers that I speak to about confidence have misconceptions that hold them back.

They think that confidence is an attribute that they cannot choose to seek and acquire. They think it's something that descends on an athlete, like a revelation from above, after he's performed perfectly for a long time.

Sometimes, a player struggling with this kind of misconception will ask me which comes first, confidence or success. They understand that a player cannot win tournaments without confidence. But they think that you have to win tournaments before you can get confidence.

If that were true, no one would ever win a tournament for the first time.

In fact, anyone can develop confidence if he or she goes about it properly. Confidence isn't something you're born with or something you're given. You control it. Confidence is what you think about yourself and your golf game.

Confidence at the level of any single shot is nothing more than thinking about your ball going to the target. If you're thinking about the ball going to the target, you're confident.

A lot of golfers find this too simple. They have good educations. They've learned how to analyze and question. They want to apply what they know about probability and statistics.

This kind of person might engage me in the following argument:

"Doc, are you confident when you stand over a forty-foot putt that you're going to make it?"

"Yes," I reply.

"Well, then, would you bet me your house that you'll make it?"

"No."

"Then how can you say you're confident?"

The answer is that while I wouldn't bet my house, that doesn't mean I'm not confident.

Being confident doesn't mean that I don't know that 2 percent is a good average on 40-foot putts. It means that when I'm standing over a 40-foot putt, no one is asking me to bet my house, and I'm not thinking about averages. I'm thinking about putting the ball in the hole. And that's all I'm thinking about.

Great athletes think this way. It would never occur to one of them to ask me whether I would bet my house on a 40-foot putt.

People would understand this better, I think, if confidence guaranteed success. It doesn't. Standing on the tee and thinking about your drive going to the target doesn't guarantee that it will go there. It only enhances the chances. If it guaranteed success, people would more readily get the idea. But they try thinking confidently, and as soon as a shot doesn't succeed, they think, "Well, that doesn't work."

But look at it another way. If you're not thinking about your drive going to the target, what are you thinking about? Obviously, you're thinking about it going somewhere else—into a lake, maybe.

And that kind of thinking definitely works, assuming you want to hit the ball in the lake. Negative thinking is almost 100 percent effective.

IN A LARGER sense, your confidence is the sum of all the thoughts you have about yourself as a golfer. You've got to think about what you want your golf game to be. You've got to think about driving it well, wedging it well, being a great bunker player, being a superb putter.

If you are a competitive player, you have to think about winning tournaments, about shooting low scores, about being able to stay cool if you get off to a rocky start and still come in with a good number.

I frequently tell touring players that when they're off the

course, if they can't think about playing great golf, they shouldn't think about golf at all.

By its nature, golf will try to sap your confidence. On every round, even the best golfer will mishit some shots. Over the course of a year, even the best golfer will lose more tournaments than he wins. So, maintaining confidence in golf is like swimming against a current. You have to work hard to stay where you are.

I tell players to try to feel that their confidence is increasing over the course of every round, every tournament and every season. I want them to feel that they are looser and more decisive on the eighteenth tee than they were on the first. I want them to feel more capable of going low on Sunday than they did on Thursday. I want them to feel more likely to win the last tournament of the season than they did in the first. As golfers grow in skills and experience, they must make certain that their confidence grows along with them.

They can do this if they learn to be selective about their thoughts and their memories. They have to learn to monitor their thinking and ask themselves whether an idea that springs to mind is likely to help them or hurt them in the effort to grow more confident.

If it won't help them, they have to make a conscious choice to put that thought out of their mind and turn to one that will enhance their confidence. They have to focus on what they want to happen, be it a particular shot or an entire career. Everyone thinks this way some of the time. Doing it consistently is a habit that requires disciplined effort.

This is what Nick Price has learned to do over the past few years. Nowadays, he tells me, the only thoughts that enter his mind on a golf course are thoughts about what he wants to do —where he wants to place his tee shot, where he wants his approach to land, and how he wants his putts to fall. The prospect of hitting a drive into the woods or running a putt way past the hole simply does not occur to him.

It can sound a little bit like self-deception. But it isn't. It is simply the way that great athletes, or successful people in any field, have trained themselves to think.

13.

....

What Mark Twain and
Fred Couples Have in Common

....
....
....

MARK TWAIN WAS not, as far as I know, much of a golfer. But he had an insight that can help any golfer develop confidence and play better.

The inability to forget, Twain said, is infinitely more devastating than the inability to remember.

Golfers, after they've played for a while, have a vast store of memories that can affect the way they play.

They've hit long, straight drives that rose majestically against an azure sky and dropped to earth in the middle of a clipped, green fairway. They've struck irons that covered the flagstick all the way and settled softly on the green. They've chipped in from the fringe. They've hit 40-foot putts and watched them snake across an undulating green and die in the cup.

They've also topped drives that barely made it off the tee.

They've shanked 7-irons out of bounds. They've left sand shots in a trap. And they've watched, horrified, as putts rolled on past a hole forever.

The question is, as you stand over a ball and prepare to hit it, which shots do you choose to remember?

A lot of players tell me they don't choose—that the memories of bad shots jump, unbidden, into their mind. Others say they have realistic memories, that they recall both the bad and the good.

But a golfer can indeed choose. Free will enables him to develop the kind of memory that promotes good shotmaking: a short-term memory for failure and a long-term memory for success. A golfer can learn to forget the bad shots and remember the good ones.

One way is to permit yourself to enjoy your good shots.

People tend to remember best those events in their lives that are associated with strong emotions, like the birth of a child or the death of a parent.

The problem is that many golfers allow themselves to get very angry at bad shots. That helps plant the memory of the bad shot strongly in their minds.

These same players tend to get very little joy or satisfaction from their good shots. They take them as routine events that cause no particular excitement.

If they thought about it, though, they would realize that a great golf shot is a thing of beauty. They would savor it and celebrate it.

I encourage players to do that. It will help make the game more enjoyable. It will help make the memory of good shots stronger.

Second, golfers often have a problem of perception. If a

player, facing a tee shot, starts to remember shots she's hit out of bounds, is she being realistic? Or is she being unduly harsh on herself?

If she thought about it, she'd probably remember that she's hit far more tee shots in bounds than out of bounds during the course of her golfing career. Remembering one of the good shots, therefore, would be far more realistic than remembering a shot that sliced out of bounds.

But golfers, particularly high-handicappers, often perceive themselves too negatively. They allow the bad shots to dominate their memories.

Good golfers, I've found, frequently have a selective memory that helps them.

The night before the final round of the Masters in 1992, I had dinner with a group of players and teachers that included Fred Couples, who went on to win the tournament.

Fred is not a player I've worked with, but he asked me that night what I thought about his mental game.

"I don't know," I said. "It looks pretty solid to me. What do you try to do?"

"Well, you know, when I come up to a shot, I just pull up my sleeves and shrug my shoulders to try to get them relaxed," Fred said. "And then I try to remember the best shot I ever hit in my life with whatever club I have in my hand. Is that okay?"

"I think that will do just fine, Freddy," I said. "Just fine."

14.

Fighting Through Fear

SEVERAL YEARS AGO, Brad Faxon began talking to me about a difficult challenge. Brad had begun to fear his driver.

Brad is one of the most successful young players on the PGA Tour. He's not overwhelmingly long, but he can hit a drive 280 yards. He's very accurate with his irons. He's a fearless wedge player who will make a long, loose swing to flop the ball onto the green in a tight situation and give it a chance to go into the hole. He's one of the best putters I've seen. And he has an ideal temperament for golf. He's intelligent and easygoing. He loves the game and he likes the people associated with it.

After he graduated from Furman in 1983, Brad quickly established himself as a professional, and by 1985 he was an exempt player on the Tour. Despite this success, he started to have vivid, disquieting thoughts about drivers, or, more precisely, what might happen to the ball after he hit it with a driver. These thoughts occurred not only on the tee. They might come to him at night in his sleep. They might come to him as he sat at the dinner table with his wife. Usually, he could see the golf ball flying 50 yards off course to the right, into trouble or out of bounds, even though his natural shot is a draw.

These thoughts became so persistent that he could no longer stand on a tee with a driver in his hands and even come close to believing that the ball would go to his target. In that mental state, his game off the tee inevitably suffered. In stressful situations, on narrow driving holes, he tightened up and lost his rhythm. If he mishit a driver, it was as if someone had punched him in the solar plexus. All the air, all the energy left his body.

It's important to differentiate between fear and nervousness. Nervousness is a physical state. It's sweat on the palms, adrenaline in the bloodstream. There's nothing wrong with it—it can even help a golfer.

Fear is a mental state. It's being afraid of making a mistake when you swing the club. Fear causes golfers to try to guide or steer the ball, rather than swing freely. That doesn't work. Swinging freely makes the ball go straight. Swinging carefully causes disasters. To play his best, a golfer has to feel that once he's aligned himself and picked his target, it's as if he doesn't care where the ball goes. He is going to trust his swing and let it go.

If fear could plague a golfer as talented and successful as Brad Faxon, it could certainly debilitate the average golfer. And it does.

I've talked to players who can't look at a downhill putt without thinking that they could roll it 10 feet past. They make ugly jabs at the ball. I've talked to players who can't look at a pitch shot over a bunker without thinking about dumping it into the sand.

They chunk a lot of wedges. And there are many, like Brad Faxon, who get fearful when they put a driver in their hands.

On the professional circuit, there have been prominent players whose careers were totally derailed by fear. One year they were contending in major championships. The next year they were staying at home, unwilling even to risk exposing their fear in a tournament.

Sometimes I wish there were a quick, simple answer for them, a psychological parlor trick that would banish their fears and allow them to hit their best shots. There isn't, at least not in most cases. Fighting through fear can take a lot of patient effort. But a golfer who learns to do it has given himself an invaluable lesson.

In Brad's case, we began by trying to decide whether his problem was mental or mechanical. He decided that it was some of both.

There were a few subtle mechanical changes he decided to make in his swing with the driver, changes having largely to do with his posture and his release. He went to work with a teaching pro to make the necessary adjustments.

With a lot of players, this would have been as far as they went. They would have proceeded to try to beat the problem to death on the practice range, hitting bucket after bucket of balls in an effort to fix their mechanics.

But the fact was that even before he made those mechanical changes, Brad could always hit the driver fairly well on the practice range. That suggested that his problem lay mainly in his mind.

We didn't waste time trying to figure out why he was getting these fearful flashes. Anyone who has played golf for a while has inevitably hit some monstrous slices or hooks off the tee.

Images of those shots remain buried in the memory, capable of springing into a golfer's consciousness at the worst possible moments. The fact was, they were springing into Brad's mind. Why they were was hardly relevant.

We reviewed some fundamental ideas. First and foremost, we talked about how free will controls thought. Any golfer can decide what he wants to think about as he contemplates a shot.

So we worked hard on getting Brad to think of what he wanted to happen with the driver rather than what he didn't want to happen. We talked about picking a target and visualizing the ball going to that target. We talked about making this the centerpiece of a mental routine that Brad would repeat on every shot, particularly tee shots.

But it wasn't that easy. Brad still could not make himself feel certain that the ball would go to the target when he hit it with a driver. He needed something to fall back on while he worked on vanquishing his fear.

So for a long time, Brad hit lots of 3-woods off the tee. I told him that whenever he felt doubt or fear about hitting a driver, he should leave it in the bag and hit a 3-wood or a 1-iron instead.

Fortunately, Brad hits an excellent 3-wood. Moreover, the rest of his game—his irons, his chipping and wedging, and his putting—helped him compensate for the loss of distance off the tee. For several years, he was able to stay high on the money list while rarely using a driver.

This didn't really surprise me. Most amateurs, watching the professionals play golf on television, notice their length off the tee first of all. It's glamorous. It's masculine. The weekend players get the idea that this length with the driver is the key to shooting low scores. But the driver is the toughest club to hit consistently. It mercilessly exposes swing flaws and thinking flaws. A lot of weekend players ruin their games with it. They think they have to hit it, and hit it a long way. When they don't, or don't hit it straight, they get tense and mechanical. Their tee shots get worse, and the rest of their game frequently comes apart as well.

In truth, while length off the tee is desirable, it's not nearly as important as keeping the ball in play and chipping and putting well, as Brad demonstrated. Weekend players who have trouble driving would do well to emulate him, hitting a 3-wood or a long iron off the tee and developing a short game they can score with. This would enable them to feel, from the beginning of every hole, that they were following their mental routines and feeling certain about every shot before they swung the club.

Of course, Brad did not want to spot the competition 40 yards off the tee indefinitely. He continued to work hard on thinking about hitting the ball where he wanted it to go. Using a 3-wood helped him maintain this habit. Gradually, he began to be able to do it more often with the driver.

He worked at this all day, not just at the golf course. I told him that he should either think about driving the ball well or not think about it at all, and he made it a habit to think about hitting long, beautiful drives. We made some audio tapes that he could play in the car in which I reminded him of great drives he had hit in critical situations. He tried to develop a long-term memory for his good drives and a short-term memory for the bad ones.

It helped as well that Brad retained a sense of humor about the whole thing. His caddie, Cubby Burke, is an imaginative and irreverent kidder who could have matched insults with the regulars at the Algonquin Round Table, provided, that is, that the Round Table permitted certain epithets common to the golf course. Brad had the good sense not to restrain Cubby, but to let himself be teased. Laughing at the problem helped put it in perspective.

By the time Brad first qualified for the Masters he had, over the course of several years, made a lot of progress. But his Masters debut made him all the more anxious to be done with his driver anxiety once and for all. Augusta National, with its absence of rough, its reachable par fives, and its long par fours, favors the long hitter. Brad was eager to do well his first time out.

The night before the tournament began, we had dinner in the house he had rented for himself and his family. After dinner, we took a walk down the dark, narrow, tree-lined street. I told him to imagine teeing a ball in the street, hitting it with a driver, blasting it straight between the trees and then drawing it into the house at the end of the block.

"Hopefully," I added, "no one will be watching through the windows."

Brad laughed and took a swing in the shadows. Yes, he said, he could see that shot.

He did it a few more times. He laughed some more. Each imaginary shot was perfect. I told him that the only difference on the golf course the next day would be the presence of a ball and a club. His body and mind could work just as well then as they did on that darkened street, unless he let the ball intimidate him.

With that thought in mind, he played well in his first Masters. He felt that he had turned a corner, and in 1992, he won two tournaments.

He learned what all successful athletes sooner or later learn. Courage is fear turned inside out. It is impossible to be courageous if at first you weren't afraid.

Finally, Brad did something that I can take no credit for. He moved from Florida back to his native Rhode Island. He started practicing and playing, between tournaments, at the courses he grew up on, Rhode Island Country Club and Metacomet. He played with friends from high-school days. This change of scenery helped him recapture the attitude toward driving the ball he had had when he was fourteen or fifteen years old, when he couldn't wait to walk onto the tee and bust one. As a kid, he had driven the ball fearlessly. Back home, he completed the process of learning to think that way again.

Nowadays, Brad's biggest problem is the opposite of the old one. He loves hitting the driver again, and he steps onto every tee looking for a reason to pull it out of the bag. Sometimes he uses it when the situation calls for a 3-wood or an iron.

That, however, doesn't strike him as such a bad problem to have.

15.

What I Learned from
Seve Ballesteros

....
....
....

A COUPLE OF summers ago, Seve Ballesteros walked up to me at the Westchester Classic and introduced himself. Seve had not been playing well for a year or so.

"Nickie Price says I need to talk to you," Seve began abruptly. "He said you'll teach me how to win again. He said what you teach is the future of golf."

I was flattered, but not so much that I was not startled by Seve Ballesteros admitting that he had lost the knowledge of how to win.

"Once," Seve went on, glumly, "*I* was the future of golf. All I ever did for years is what I think you teach. I just saw myself in my mind winning golf tournaments. I saw myself making the shots. I saw myself winning. The year I won the Masters by seven or eight shots, I knew I would win it before the plane landed in America. The only problem was that I walked up the eighteenth fairway without any joy, because I had known I would win before the tournament started."

I winked at him. "Well, I could certainly teach you how to get happy and party."

But Seve was not in a mood to banter. He wanted to explain himself.

It turned out that, in Seve, personality and environment had combined to produce a golfing artist. He grew up poor in Spain, and like Hagen, Nelson, Sarazen and Hogan, he got into the game as a caddie. He started playing with a few mismatched clubs, and he competed ferociously from the outset.

From the beginning, Seve had focused his energy not on his swing, which he picked up instinctively. He was always concerned with the ball, with making the ball move in such a way that it went into the hole. He was the kind of kid who might walk into a sand trap with a cast-off 7-iron and experiment until he found ways to get the ball up to the hole with it.

He had a natural instinct for thinking right. When he went to sleep at night, he saw himself making great shots and winning tournaments.

When he practiced, he told me, he would almost immediately have all of his clubs strewn on the ground beside him. He was not the type to hit one club over and over, seeking to groove a swing. He played imaginary holes on the range, inventing different shots to fit the circumstances his mind conjured up. He might imagine a par five, and hit a driver and a 2-iron. If the 2-iron drifted a little left, he'd pull out his wedge and practice a flop shot.

In his first years as a professional, Seve said, he'd had a feeling of immense control. He felt sometimes as if he controlled not only himself and his ball, but the galleries and his opponents as well.

"You know," he said, "when I first came to America, if I hit the ball in the rough, I didn't care."

He crouched down like a golfer peering under the low branches of a tree at a distant green.

"I just looked for a way, an opening. I didn't care that there was a tree there. I just found the opening, hit the ball over the tree, or around it, or under it, and got the ball in the hole. When I saw an American player hit the ball in the rough and then chip out into the fairway, I laughed. I thought, 'How can they beat me if they do that?'

"Then, around the green, I saw that a lot of them hit a putter from the fringe. They said that if they missed with the putter, they left the ball closer than if they missed with a wedge. I thought that was silly. I used a wedge. I never thought I would miss."

Now, he went on sadly, he had started to resemble those golfers he used to scorn. He pitched sideways out of the rough. He used a putter from the fringe. His whole attitude toward the game had changed and all the joy was gone.

"It used to be that I would come to the eighteenth hole and be sad because there was no more golf left to play," he said. "Now I come to the ninth hole and I'm sad because I still have nine to go. I hate golf like this. I don't want to keep playing if it feels like this."

As we talked, it became apparent that Seve's game had gone sour when he tried to change from the intuitive, imaginative and ball-oriented attitude of his youth to a mechanical, swing-oriented approach. A sincere desire to improve had prompted him to do it, but he had found that it was not easy—and perhaps impossible—to go from being an artist to being a scientist.

"I wanted very much to win the U.S. Open," he said. "People

would tell me that I would have to get a much better, more consistent swing if I wanted to win on a U.S. Open course."

People are always giving unsolicited lessons and tips to leading professionals like Seve. They want to take some of the credit for his successes. In his desire to win an Open, Seve bought the idea that he needed to restructure his swing, to make it more mechanically flawless. He forgot that course management, a stellar short game, good putting and patience win Opens. Of these, the only quality he might have lacked was patience.

So he set out to perfect his swing. He took lessons from some of the game's most renowned teachers of golf mechanics. His swing doctors persuaded him that if he practiced hard enough, he could incorporate half a dozen or more separate changes into his swing and find the Nirvana where all balls are perfectly struck. And periodically, on the range, all of these changes would fall into place and Seve would start hitting beautiful shots.

The trouble was that all of this work on the swing changed his attitude toward the game. Now, if he hit a drive into the rough, his mind did not click into thoughts of how to get the ball through the trees and into the hole. It clicked instead into thoughts of swing mechanics. He felt that he understood his swing now, and he should be able to fix it on the course and make the next shot great.

It didn't work.

"If I hit one bad shot, I started trying to do all things my teacher had been telling me about. Things just got worse and worse," he said. Eventually, he added, the tendency to think mechanically had infected his short game.

He stopped winning tournaments and, after a while, he stopped enjoying the game.

In a corner of his mind, Seve knew what had gone wrong. He

understood that he couldn't think of all those swing changes and still hit the ball.

But then he discovered that it was not easy to go back to the old, instinctive way of thinking on the course.

I told Seve that he had to find his way back to the old Seve. He had to learn again to trust his athletic ability. He had to recapture the attitude of the young Spanish caddie, navigating the golf course with a handful of cast-off clubs, inventing shots to get the ball into the hole.

I talked to him a little about how the body and brain work best together when an athlete simply looks at a target and reacts to it, rather than thinking about the mechanics of his movement.

That struck a chord with Seve.

"You know, when I was a little boy, a caddie, we pitched pennies in the caddie yard. We'd put a club down on the ground and pitch pennies to the club. No one could touch me at it. I was the best. Sometimes, now, I lie in bed in the hotel and throw things at that—what do you call it in the corner?—the trash can. And I never miss. I don't know how I do it. I just do it, like you say."

I was only telling Seve something he had realized himself at some level. He knew he had to recapture the confident focus on the hole that had characterized his best golf. He knew he had to go back to being an artist rather than trying to be a scientist.

"I know what you tell me is right," Seve said. "I know I have to go back to being Seve. But be patient. It's going to take a while. I think I will. But now I have these thoughts in my head, and I can't get rid of them."

He told me that when he stepped on a golf course, where once he had felt completely in control, he now felt lost and in jeopardy. "It feels," he said, "like I'm stepping on clouds and I'm going to fall through."

My conversations with Seve reminded me of how a player can get lost trying to improve. It's not enough to decide to get better and to be willing to work hard at it. A player has to judge carefully whether the improvement nostrums he's being offered are right for him.

Some players with a more natural mechanical bent—the scientists—might have been able to incorporate the changes that Seve tried to make in his swing without losing the ability to trust their mechanics on the golf course and remember that the objective is to get the ball in the hole.

But others, who play by feel—the artists—can hurt themselves trying to do it. Our conversation showed that even a golfer who has won eighty tournaments around the world has to take care to maintain and enhance his mental game, his confidence and his trust no matter what he is doing with his swing. Even such a golfer as Seve needs to find a teacher who recognizes that too much mechanical advice can be harmful.

This is all the more important for amateurs who play once or twice a week. They need to keep their swings simple and their confidence high. They must learn to resist the kind of temptation that can lead to loss of confidence, temptation often garbed as well-meaning advice.

Most golfers assume that once they learn how to think confidently, they can fiddle with their mental approach to the game. They believe they can always go back to the attitude they once had.

But, as Seve learned, it's not always that easy.

I think Seve is on his way back. He's recognized his problem and he's dealing honestly with it. Periodically, I scan the European golf results to see whether he's broken through and started winning again. Recently, I noticed that he had.

As long as he has his dreams and his passion, I expect that he will keep coming back.

16.

Conservative Strategy,

Cocky Swing

....
....
....

PERHAPS NO SINGLE shot has misled more golfers than the drive Arnold Palmer hit to the first green in the final round of the U.S. Open at Cherry Hills in 1960.

The first at Cherry Hills then was a 346-yard par four with trees down the left side, a ditch on the right, and thick, U.S. Open rough in front of the green. The course, outside Denver, is a mile high, and balls fly farther at altitude. Palmer decided he could drive the green. In the fourth round, he proved it.

Virtually every American golfer heard the story of that tee shot and how it launched Palmer on the way to a closing 65 that overcame a seven-stroke deficit and won him his only Open title. Palmer's final round burned into the minds of a golfing generation the idea that real men, and real winners, play aggressive, even reckless golf.

But not many people remember what Palmer's effort to drive

the green produced in the first three rounds of that Open: one par, a bogey, and a double-bogey, thanks to drivers hit slightly awry. In other words, Palmer was three over par for No. 1 when he started the fourth round. The final birdie he got by driving the green meant that he had played the hole in two over for the tournament.

Suppose he had decided to play the hole differently that week, hitting a 2-iron off the tee and setting up a wedge into the green. He would, most likely, have done no worse than par each round. Quite possibly he would have sunk a birdie putt or two.

He wouldn't have needed to close with a 65 to win.

That 1960 Open was one of the first to demonstrate an unfortunate truth: listening to television golf commentators can be hazardous to your game.

Television producers want the broadcast to be exciting. They want the drama of bold, reckless shots and swashbuckling players. So when they see a player gamble the way Palmer did, they glorify him. People listen to the broadcasts, and they get the idea that bold, reckless shots pay off.

They don't. At least not often enough to make them worthwhile.

The key to successful strategy and a confident swing for golfers at every level is, instead, quite the opposite.

Hit the shot you know you can hit, not the shot Arnold Palmer would hit, nor even the shot you think you ought to be able to hit.

I teach a conservative strategy and a cocky swing. You want to play each hole in such a way that you're confident you can execute each shot you attempt. That gives you a cocky swing, which is another way of saying that you swing aggressively, that you swing with trust. It produces your best results.

The opposite approach would be a bold strategy and a tentative swing. A bold strategy would have you attempting shots you are not confident you can hit. That leads very quickly to tentative swings, and tentative swings produce bad shots. Bad execution of bold shots produces very high scores.

What does this mean in practice?

A great story from the literature of golf illustrates the point.

The late Tommy Armour won all the major championships available to a professional golfer in his day—the U.S. Open in 1927, the British Open in 1931, and the PGA in 1930. But at that time, golf tournaments paid the winner a thousand dollars or so. A professional golfer who aspired to a decent standard of living had to know how to make money in other ways—in short, to hustle. And Tommy Armour liked to live well.

After his competitive career ended, Armour spent his winters at a posh club in Boca Raton, Florida, giving lessons in golf and gamesmanship to the swells. He took their money in the mornings, giving swing lessons. And he took it in the afternoons, playing exorbitant Nassaus.

"What do you take me for? Jack Benny?" Armour would fulminate when someone on the first tee suggested slightly lower stakes.

One winter day in the locker room, Armour overheard a pupil of his offering to bet some friends that he could break 90, a feat that the pupil had theretofore never threatened to accomplish. Armour's keen instinct for a sure thing was aroused.

Armour offered to back his pupil in the wager, on one condition: that Armour be allowed to walk the course with him during the round and offer advice.

With the stakes set, and set high, the match commenced. The first hole was a long par four. Armour's pupil wound up and sliced a long drive into the rough to the right of the first fairway. They walked to the ball and eyed the green, about 170 yards away, elevated, guarded by a couple of deep traps. The pupil pulled out his 5-iron.

"Put the five-iron back," Armour said. "You're going to play an eight-iron to the fairway thirty yards short of the green and a little left. Then you're going to chip up through the opening to the green. The worst you'll make is five. If you go for the green and mishit that five-iron just a little bit, you're looking at six or seven."

The pupil was smart enough to do as he was told. He played the 8-iron to the spot Armour indicated. He chipped up. He sank the putt for his par. He went on to shoot 79. And Tommy Armour won enough money to live a good while longer in the style to which he was accustomed.

What Armour had done, of course, was to give his student a temporary brain transplant. With Armour making the strategy choices, the student played only shots that were well within his physical capabilities. He aimed at specific targets that Armour selected for him. He felt calm, confident and decisive. He stopped worrying about his swing mechanics, assuming that Armour would correct any flaws that needed correcting. And by doing those things, by acquiring a conservative strategy and a cocky swing, he shot a score he had previously only dreamed of.

This principle applies to golf at the highest levels as well. Tom Watson, in his final round at the 1992 U.S. Open, demonstrated it.

Playing the par-five 18th hole, Watson hit a 3-wood onto the fairway and then a 7-iron, leaving him a full 9-iron to the green. The broadcast crew, expecting his second shot to stop much closer to the green, thought momentarily that he had flubbed it. Of course, he hadn't. Normally, he said later, he laid up closer, with a 5-iron. But earlier in the round, he had partially mishit two short fairway sand-wedge shots. He wanted a full 9-iron into the green because he didn't think he would feel confident with a wedge, particularly a partial wedge.

A lot of golfers, facing that situation, would have tried to bash a driver and a long iron and lay up close to the green. They would have told themselves that they simply have to be able to hit a fairway wedge if they want to consider themselves real golfers. Not Watson. He was perfectly content to leave the wedges in his bag until he had a chance to do some postround practice and restore his confidence with them. So he altered his strategy slightly to give him the shot he wanted. But he altered it in the conservative direction.

He had, in other words, a conservative strategy and a cocky swing.

17.

Game Plan

No FOOTBALL OR basketball coach whom I've ever heard of would send his team into competition without a game plan. Coaches in those sports recognize that an intelligent game plan can take advantage of a team's strengths and camouflage its weaknesses. More important, a good game plan makes the mental side of the game easier. Players don't have to make as many impromptu, possibly emotional decisions. They can instead execute decisions made in advance, calmly, outside the heat of competition.

The same considerations apply to golf:

You must play every significant round with a game plan.

Amateur golfers, particularly high-handicappers, frequently don't understand this. They play spontaneously, making up strategy on the fly. As a result, they make more bad decisions.

A good professional never plays a tournament round without

first examining the course and preparing a plan to play it. The plan encompasses target and club selection for each tee shot, the preferred landing area on every green, and hazards to be avoided. It envisions responses to rain, wind and other weather variables.

The professional plans all this ahead of time because he wants to do as little analyzing and improvising as possible once he's on the course. He wants to leave his mind clear and free to focus on each target.

Once in a while a player has to play a round on a course totally new to him, without time to inspect it beforehand. In such cases, a golfer has to improvise. He should look at hole diagrams on the scorecard, ask a caddie, or ask a member with local knowledge. Even a plan made up at each tee is better than no plan at all. But whenever possible, plan in advance.

The best way to prepare a plan is to walk or mentally review each hole backward. Standing on the green and looking back toward the tee usually reveals much more about a hole than standing on the tee and looking at the green. It shows more of the tricks and deceptions that the architect may have built into the hole. And it forces you to think strategically about where you want your ball to land on the green, what club would be best for landing it there, and what kind of tee shot will set this up.

Consider perhaps the most familiar stretch of holes in tournament golf, Nos. 10–13 at Augusta National, the holes encompassing Amen Corner. What do you learn from examining each hole backward? This is what I see when I walk them with a player preparing for the Masters:

No. 10 is a long, downhill par four, a slight dogleg left, 485 yards from the tournament tees. Standing on the 10th green and facing the tee, you immediately notice that the green itself slopes to the left into a downslope that is very hard to chip back from. Next, you notice how tough the shot can be from the bunker that protects the front right corner of the green; you might have as much as 50 yards of carry from the far end of the bunker to the far end of the green.

For a professional, the biggest discovery gleaned from standing on the green is how much the hole favors a tee shot played down the left side. This isn't so apparent from the tee. But from the green you see that the downslope in the fairway is much more significant on the left side. A drive drawn around the corner and down the left side can make the hole play almost a hundred yards shorter than a tee shot blocked down the right side.

Hitting the left side of the fairway leaves a professional with a 6- or 7-iron, while the approach from the right can be a long iron or a fairway wood from a sidehill lie that makes you feel as if you're standing on your ear. So, for a professional or a first-class amateur with good length, the game plan is very likely going to be to draw a drive down the left side.

Every game plan, of course, must be tailored to the individual's strengths and preferences. It must be based on an honest appraisal of a player's skills, and it can change from one year to the next, or one round to the next, depending on changes in those skills. I would never prescribe to a player the strategy he or she ought to use on a given hole. If one of my players told me he just felt better hitting the ball down the right side at No. 10, that would be fine with me. My concern is that the player has a plan, that he believes in the plan, and that he follows the plan.

For a typical member at Augusta National, or an amateur lucky enough to be invited to play there, the calculations on No. 10 would be somewhat different. He would still take note of the leftward slope of the green, especially if he likes to putt from below the hole. He would definitely pay attention to the potential problem caused by the right bunker. He would want to avoid at all costs a long, faded approach shot that fell short, slid into that bunker and left him with perhaps the most difficult of all shots for amateurs, the long bunker shot to a green that slopes away.

He would also take note of the trees on either side of the fairway, trees that rarely come into play at the Masters, but which could certainly threaten to catch a drive a weekend player might hit, particularly if he swung hard, trying for distance. Finally, he would note the large bunker in the middle of the fairway, about a hundred yards short of the green. It rarely affects a Masters golfer, but if the amateur laid up, he would be safest to lay up short of that bunker.

From these observations, the intelligent amateur might well conclude that he must play this hole as a short par five rather than a long par four. He would want to hit his first ball somewhere into the fairway and his second shot short of the big fairway trap, a total distance of perhaps 360 yards. That would leave him an easy wedge or 9-iron to the green, with a chance to sink a putt for a par and a realistic plan to make no worse than five on the hole. That's not bad, considering that the Masters field averages about 4.2 strokes here.

By working backward, the amateur can then make an informed decision about the club to use off the tee. If he merely stood on the tee, without a plan, he would probably decide to bust his driver as far as he could, given the length of the hole. But by working the hole backward and planning a strategy, he might come to a different conclusion. If he can hit a fairway wood or even a 3-iron somewhere into the fairway, he has only a comfortable mid-iron left to his lay-up position. The obvious call, if he wants a conservative strategy and a cocky swing, is to leave the driver in the bag and play something he knows will get the ball into the fairway, 200 yards or so out. Then he can count on a 6- or 7-iron to the lay-up spot.

If he risks the driver and hits it well, say, 240 yards down the middle, what has he gained? He's still looking at a 245-yard shot to the green, (assuming, for the sake of illustration, that he's playing this hole from the tournament tees). This shot is beyond the capability of most amateurs. If he misses the second shot right, he's looking at that difficult long bunker shot. If he decides to lay up, all he's accomplished with his driver is to reduce his lay-up club from a 6-iron to a 9-iron. The reward does not justify the risk.

The same goes for most amateurs playing long par fours on any course. A lot of them have no chance of reaching par-four holes that are over 430 yards. They could easily reach the greens on all these holes with a couple of smooth 5-irons and a wedge. Yet they consistently pull the driver out of the bag and get themselves into trouble, turning a hole that could be a routine bogey and occasional par into a 6, a 7, or an 8.

Too many players at all levels try to rip a driver on nearly every tee. A professional might tell you that he truly has confidence in his driver. And sometimes that's justified. A Tom Kite or a Nick Price can play a precision shot with a driver. But a weekend player, if he or she is honest, will generally admit that the driver comes out of the bag because the driver is fun. It appeals to the ego to hit, occasionally, a drive that impresses the rest of the foursome. So even if he recognizes that he might score better if he never carried a driver, he keeps using it.

If that's what you want to do, fine. Just don't get angry when you get punished for it, because you're going to get punished severely on most courses. Instead of a third wedge, you might want to carry a chain saw.

If your objective is to shoot the best score you can, you might do well to remember why Jack Nicklaus, Ben Hogan and Nick Faldo hit lots of 1-irons and 3-woods off the tee. Even if the longest club you can hit confidently onto the fairway is a 5-iron, you'd be better off using it if your purpose is to score.

This is doubly true on short par fours. A good architect will tempt a player on one of these short holes to hit the ball a long way, thinking to drive the green or set up a very short second shot. But the architect, if he's good, will build lots of trouble into the hole where even slightly errant drives would land. The smart choice is usually to hit an iron or fairway wood off the tee, leaving a full wedge for the second shot.

No. 11 AT Augusta is another long par four, 455 yards. Standing on its green, the first thing you notice is the little pond in front of the left side of the green. This will influence the way you play the hole. No matter where the flag is, and on Sunday at the Masters it is always near the pond, you want your second shot to stay safely away from the water.

This might seem, at first blush, to be negative thinking. Why not ignore the pond and fire at the flag, even if it's on the left side? Isn't that positive thinking?

Positive thinking, in my opinion, does not mean taking a rip at every risky shot the course presents. It is, rather, the development and execution of an intelligent strategy that weighs risks and rewards and gives a player a chance to shoot his best possible score.

I tell my professional players that going for the flag depends on the distance. With a wedge in their hands, they should always go for it. Indeed, they should go for the hole. No one makes it to the Tour without being at least that good with the wedge. Between 120 and 170 yards is a gray area for most professionals. They must consider the wind, the speed of the greens, how they feel, and the potential penalty for a slightly missed shot before they decide whether to aim for the pin. If, for instance, the penalty for missing is likely to be no worse than a routine bunker shot, especially from the uniform, groomed bunkers at Augusta, a professional might go for the pin. If the penalty is a wet ball and a stroke penalty, he'll probably aim for the middle of the green. From 170 yards out or farther, I advise professionals to always shoot for the fattest or safest part of the green, regardless of where the flag is. Once in a while, I see someone knock it close to a tight pin from 200 or 250 yards. Invariably, the television announcer will praise his boldness for going for the flag from that distance. In fact, what usually happened is that the player aimed for the middle of the green and mishit it.

On No. 11, the safe side is obviously the right side. In fact, closer observation of the green area shows that there is a spacious area of manicured fairway grass to the right of the green. This is the area from which Larry Mize chipped in to beat Greg Norman in their 1987 playoff. You could even putt from there if you trusted your putter.

The professionals who get in trouble with the pond on No. 11 are usually players who don't feel confident about their putting and chipping. They are afraid they will need three to get down unless they get their second shots close to the pin. You can be a genius at course management if you're really cocky with your wedge and putter.

For weekend players looking backward at No. 11, the calculations would again be somewhat different. The hole would be too long for some of them to reach in two, and they would do best to devise a plan for the first two shots that would leave them their most comfortable pitching distance. Their target as they approach the green would depend on their personal threshold distance. Inside the threshold distance, they would go for the flag. Beyond it, they would shoot for the right side of the green, taking the pond out of play. Looking at a long iron into the green, an amateur might well aim for the right edge, planning to rely on his short game to get up and down if he hits the fairway area to the right of the green. This strategy takes the pond out of play.

No. 12, although only 155 yards long, is another hole that rewards a backward examination. From the green, the perils of Rae's Creek are more apparent than they are from the tee. The green, which simply looks wide from the tee, shows itself to be terribly shallow once you're standing on it. And it is easier to see that the creek, which looks from the tee to flow perpendicular to the line of the shot, in fact bends away from the tee on the right side of the green. This means that there is almost no margin for error on the right. A few yards too long, and the ball is bunkered, raising the possibility that the ensuing sand shot will roll back over the green and into the water. A few yards too short, and the ball is lost, unless you are Fred Couples in 1992 and the gods are smiling down on you. (And you have the ability and presence of mind to get it up and down from the bank as he did.)

Therefore, most professionals always aim for the left center of the green at No. 12, where the margin for error is greater. Of course, the pin is always cut on the right side on Sunday, but most feel that going for it is not worth the risk.

A good game plan has to be flexible for holes like this. You can't plan on the club to use until you have a chance to assess the wind. (Of course, No. 12 is a great hole because it's so hard to figure out what the wind is doing.) When Tom Kite plans his Masters round, he will typically decide to use a 6-iron or a 7-iron at No. 12, depending on the wind. The important thing to plan on here is making a decisive club selection when the time comes. Once you make up your mind, you have to believe in your decision.

Good golf courses like Augusta National are full of sucker pin placements analogous to the right-side position on No. 12. A good player learns to resist them. A few years ago, when the PGA Championship was being played at Shoal Creek, I was walking during a practice round with Tom Kite and Gary Player. They got to the 16th, a fairly long par three with a big green shaped liked a distended kidney. The closer section of the kidney was reasonably wide and accommodating, but the far section was very tight, guarded by sand and heavy rough. It was obvious that when the tournament started, particularly during the closing rounds, the pin would be cut in the far section and that a lot of bogeys would be made there by players trying to reach that flag with a long iron.

"I don't care where they put the pin," Player told his partners. "I'm aiming right there." And he pointed to the fat part of the green. As it turned out, he played that hole in two under par for the tournament, better than virtually everyone else in the field. He made one birdie by holing a 90-foot putt that rolled partly through the fringe. Player had, as he usually does, a smart game plan. He played conservatively and carried a cocky putter.

The weekend player's plan for No. 12 at Augusta will be the same as the professional's, except perhaps for club selection.

The hole really doesn't offer much choice. But there are longer par threes on other courses that do.

The most famous example is No. 16 at Cypress Point, which plays 220 or 230 yards from tee to green, almost all of it over the Pacific Ocean. Examining the hole backward shows an alternative route. Aim at the hulk of a dead cypress tree well to the left of the green, and the carry over the water is only 140 yards to a broad fairway. A reasonable 7-iron (assuming the wind is not blowing in your face) will leave a simple pitch of 60 or 70 yards to the green.

Which route would you take? It depends, of course, on your game. If you had a dependable club that could carry 220 yards, even into the wind, you would go for the green. But as Allister Mackenzie knew well when he designed Cypress Point, most amateurs don't consistently carry the ball that far. A lot of them might think they do, but they're probably confusing carry with total driving distance, which includes roll. And the penalty for hitting a little short at No. 16 is severe. The ball bounces off the cliff on the far side of the inlet and becomes a toy for the seals. You're still on the tee, preparing to hit your third shot.

I'm certainly not going to tell players fortunate enough to get a chance to play Cypress Point that they should not pull out their drivers or 3-woods and have a go at No. 16. But if they played the course frequently, or in competition, the intelligent plan for a lot of them would be to aim for the dead cypress tree and the fairway to the left of the green and take the safe route, playing for a possible par and a fairly certain bogey. This is not negative thinking. It's honest thinking. If you honestly assess your game and determine that you will hit the 7-iron successfully nine out of ten times and hit the driver to the green one time in ten, the risk-reward calculation is obvious. It would only be negative thinking if you then let yourself lose confidence in your ability to hit the 7-iron.

Your course might have an analogous, if less spectacular, long par three. There might be out-of-bounds markers running down one side of the hole. There might be a pond or creek in front of the green. In such cases, the smart game plan for a weekend player could be to lay up with a medium iron, pitch onto the green, and take double-bogey or triple-bogey out of the equation. On the other hand, if the hole is wide open, the smart plan might be to bang away with the driver. The point is to think about these things ahead of time, when you can make your decision coldly and rationally.

No. 13 AT Augusta, at 485 yards, is probably the toughest short par five the touring pros will see all year. I've never told a player whether his game plan should have him go for a par-five green in two or not. It's a decision that the individual has to make, based on the hole and the strengths and weaknesses of his own game. Some players hit long irons exceptionally well. Others don't. The length of the tee shot obviously plays a critical role. Most professionals' game plans for par fives establish a threshold distance. If their second shot would be shorter than, say, 230 yards, they go for it. If it is longer, they lay up.

In general, on par-five decisions, I tell players to ask themselves whether the risks they are taking in trying to reach the green in two are worth the reward. If the second shot misses the green, can it go out of bounds or into a water hazard? Or is a greenside bunker the worst penalty the course is likely to exact for a miss? I hate bumping into a player after a round and hearing him say, "God, if I had just not double-bogeyed that par five, I'd be leading." Players who carefully balance risk against reward rarely have to say that. For a professional, a birdie is or should be almost as likely from a comfortable lay-up position as it is from a spot on the edge of the green, 40 feet from the hole.

That's the calculation Chip Beck made in the 1993 Masters on another par five, No. 15. I had worked with Chip for four or five years, although we had stopped some time before this tournament. Chip has a great attitude toward the game and its adversities.

I have told him, as I tell all the players I work with, to be prepared for second-guessing. I learned playing quarterback for my high-school football team that if you call an audible and it works, fans and writers call you a genius. If it fails, they call you a dope. You have to know yourself well enough to shrug off either appellation. If Chip had gone for the green in two, sunk the eagle putt, and won the tournament, the writers and the television commentators would have canonized him. And if he hit a wood into the water or plugged it into the lip of the bunker on the right, they would have said that he got impatient and lost his composure. I tell players not to let this kind of baloney, whether positive or negative, surprise, disturb or gratify them. They should accept the fact that it comes with the territory for a contender in major championships. They should be glad that they're in that territory.

Chip was obviously very close to his threshold distance on No. 15 that Sunday. His lie was not helpful. It was downhill, on the back side of a mound, which makes it harder to control the ball. The pin was back right, meaning that if he managed to get the ball over the pond and into the bunker on the right, he'd still very likely make only a par. So he chose to lay up. It was not that he wanted to settle for par and protect second place.

He wanted the birdie. He just calculated that he had a better chance to make it using his wedge and putter. As it happened, he made par.

But, Chip made the right decision, despite what you might have heard from your newspaper's golf expert or the sports maven on the eleven o'clock news. If his wedge shot had landed a few feet shorter and he had made his birdie, those same people would have been saying what a great course manager he was and praised his patience.

Anyone who doubted Chip's nerve had obviously forgotten what happened on No. 13 a few minutes earlier. He hit a beautiful wood over Rae's Creek and into the green, stopping 25 feet away. Bernhard Langer then hit a 3-iron a foot inside him, with the same line. Chip's eagle putt lipped out. Langer, able to study the line and speed by watching Chip's ball, made his three.

That and a few other putts like it made the difference in the tournament. Langer's went in and Chip's didn't.

With all that said, No. 13 is short enough so that virtually everyone in the Masters field can reach it in two, given a decent drive. Standing on the green and looking backward helps plan how to do it. The first thing you notice is Rae's Creek, winding down the left side of the fairway and curling in front of the green. Then you notice the steep cant of the fairway in the area from which the second shot is likely to be played. The ball will be well above the golfer's feet on that shot, which may make it harder for him to hold the green. After looking at the hole this way, a lot of smart players decide not to flirt with the water on the left and to play a little right instead, toward where the spotters usually stand on this hole. The temptation on the tee is to try to burn the drive down the left side and draw it. You can set up a very short second shot this way, but you can also get into a lot of trouble.

For a professional, the most important thing for both the tee shot and the second shot is being decisive. He must pick a target, pick a club, and believe in both. I spend a lot of time prior to the Masters with my players' caddies. I tell them to support whatever club decision their players make, not allowing any doubts to slip out. In other words, if the player stands in the fairway at No. 13 and says 4-iron, and the caddie thinks the 3-iron would be better, I want the caddie to say that 4-iron is exactly what he was thinking.

For the weekend player, this kind of consideration is largely irrelevant. Even if he busts his drive 250 yards, he's still looking at a 235-yard approach over Rae's Creek. He's better off thinking about the distance from which his third shot will be most comfortable. In a lot of cases, this will not mean laying up close to the creek. It will mean laying up well back of the creek, leaving a full wedge shot in. And that raises the issue of what to hit off the tee, just as it did on No. 10. In a lot of cases, amateurs would be better off hitting a 3-wood or a long iron rather than reflexively pulling out the driver. This applies to many par fives played from the white tees, in the range of 470–520 yards. Unless a player can realistically plan on reaching the green in two, what's the point of hitting a driver?

Weekend players generally would do well to spend time practicing with a long iron or fairway wood until they have a club they know they can hit 200 yards into the fairway. It will make the game a lot easier for them.

PROBLEMS OF STRATEGY at Amen Corner, as on any good course, require detailed knowledge of yardages to solve. In recent years, with more courses posting yardages on sprinkler heads in the fairway, amateurs have tended to become complacent

about yardages, figuring that there will always be a nearby sprinkler head to tell them the distance left to the middle (or front,
depending on the course) of the green. That's true, as far as it
goes. But sprinkler heads and 150-yard markers won't give a
golfer many of the distances he needs. Only walking the course
and annotating your own scorecard will do that, and when I
talk to professional or college players, I stress the necessity of
doing so.

On many holes, for instance, you need to know the precise
distance between the tee and a particular hazard like a tree, trap
or creek, or to the corner of a dogleg. On par fives, you need to
take into account the distance from points in the tee-shot landing area to the ideal lay-up position. Unless you know these
distances, you will face an extra and unnecessary element of
doubt as you prepare to hit your shots. And doubt is the last
thing you want floating through your mind as you prepare to
hit the ball.

Your game plan must also prepare you for adversity. No matter how carefully you study the course and plan your targets,
you are not going to hit everything perfectly. And even if you
hit it perfectly, golf courses are full of bad bounces. Some of
your tee shots are going to land in fairway traps. Some of your
approach shots will also find sand. Once in a while you'll be in
the woods, and once in a while you'll be in the water.

Your plan has to prepare you for all contingencies, so you're
ready for the best happening and ready for the worst. Let's
suppose that you are about to play in a club championship, and
the 1st hole, a 370-yard par four, has a deep-lipped fairway trap
235 yards out from the tee on the left side and out-of-bounds
on the right. You decide that you'll hit a 3-wood off the tee,
aiming for the left center. You choose the 3-wood because you
can't normally hit it 235 yards and you rarely slice this club

enough to go out of bounds. Four rounds out of five, your choice will work out fine. But one round out of five you might block it right, past the white stakes. Or you might really catch it pure and see it trickle into the fairway trap.

If you haven't planned for either eventuality, you might get all upset and kick away your chances right there. But if you've prepared, you will know that in the event of an out-of-bounds tee shot the only effective thing to do is to realize that all players occasionally block a ball, forget about it, tee up a new ball, and swing more freely than you did on the first shot. In the event of hitting the fairway trap, you'll have already decided that if you're within five yards of the lip, you can't reach the green, and you'll take out a sand wedge and rely on your short game to salvage par. If you're more than five yards from the lip, you'll take out an 8-iron and go for the green. The important thing is to be prepared for both bad shots and the bad breaks the course can dish out even on good shots. When they happen, as they inevitably will, you'll maintain your equilibrium.

Doing this helped Tom Kite win the U.S. Open in 1992. Three years previously, at Oak Hill, he let a bad hole upset him. This was the 5th, and it happened when he was leading. He hit a shot in the water, pitched up, and had a putt for a bogey. As he later described it to me, he still felt positive and confident and knew he was going to make it. But two feet from the hole, the ball caught a subtle break that he hadn't foreseen and slid past. He was really shocked. Rather than mark the ball, collect himself, and adhere to his routine, he walked up to the next putt quickly and missed it. That turned the hole into a triple-bogey and really hurt his chance to win that Open.

In 1992, as he prepared for the Open at Pebble Beach, I asked Tom every day whether he was prepared to miss a two-foot putt and not let it bother him. He told me he was.

He proved it Sunday on the 4th hole. Everyone remembers the chip he holed for a birdie at No. 7 to take the lead. But to me, what happened at No. 4 was equally important.

The 4th at Pebble Beach is a very short par four, only 327 yards from the back tees. It's one of the holes a good player wants to birdie, because he knows he's likely to need that cushion as he plays the much tougher holes ahead. Tom hit two good shots at No. 4, a 4-wood and a sand wedge, but his approach hit a hard spot on the slick, wind-dried green and bounced into a bunker. He exploded out, missed his par putt, and had a tricky short putt for bogey. He missed it and took double-bogey.

But this time, he had learned his lesson and was better prepared. He never let his thoughts get ahead of his position on the course. He never let himself wonder whether those two wasted strokes had cost him his chance at the Open. He kept his attention focused tightly on every ensuing shot as it came up. He stayed with his game plan and his routine. And he won his richly deserved major championship.

YOUR GAME PLAN must always have flexibility. You must think in advance about what you will do if the wind blows strongly. In this case, you might hit more low irons off the tees into the wind rather than taking a chance on a wood hit up into the wind. You might hit a driver instead of a shorter club on a par five with the wind at your back, if the wind gives you a good chance to reach the hole in two. If it rains, or the course is soggy, your shots will get less carry and much less roll. You have to alter your plan accordingly. You may want to use longer clubs off the tee and go for more pins in marginal situations.

But in general, I recommend altering your game plan only in

a conservative direction. I don't like to see players under pressure make bolder and more aggressive choices than their plan calls for, especially in medal play. Too often, the new choice winds up costing them more strokes. Any time you're not sure, make the more conservative choice.

18.

Thriving Under Pressure

....
....
....

MOST GOLFERS TAKE up the game casually. As beginners, they're just trying to learn how to hit the ball, and their only opposition is the game itself.

But sooner or later, most move on to another level, the level of competition and pressure. They join a foursome that plays for a few dollars a side. They enter club tournaments. At higher levels, they try to make their living as professionals. And at the highest level, they try to engrave their names on the trophies awarded at major championships.

When they step up to this level, they often find that they perceive the game very differently. The grass is still green and the ball is still white. But fairways that once looked wide and inviting turn tight and menacing. Putts that once seemed short and straight start to writhe like snakes.

At their first exposure to competitive pressure, not to put too fine a point on it, a lot of players choke. They don't produce anything resembling the kind of golf they play when they're completely relaxed.

To deal with choking, let's first define it.

A golfer chokes when he lets anger, doubt, fear or some other extraneous factor distract him before a shot.

Distracted, the golfer then fails to do one or more of the things he normally does. He fails to follow his routine, particularly his mental routine. He forgets his game plan. He fails to accept his shots. Quite often under pressure, a distracting doubt or fear turns on the conscious mind. The golfer stops trusting his swing. He starts going through a checklist of errors to avoid. He gets tight and careful. When he's tight and careful, his body must work against gravity, rhythm and flow. His muscles get spastic, his feet get stiff, and he loses his natural grace and tempo. He hits a bad shot, relative to his ability.

That's all that choking really is.

It's important to dispose of a few common misconceptions.

First of all, choking is not synonymous with being nervous. The fact is that, at one time or another, all golfers are nervous. I visited Jack Nicklaus some years ago, and I remember vividly what he told me about nerves. Nicklaus wanted to be nervous. He liked being nervous. One of the symptoms that he noticed as he aged and his performance level started to decline was that he didn't get nervous often enough.

"I don't know how you play well unless you're nervous," he said. "Nowadays, I don't get nervous unless I'm in a major and in a position to win. If I could only learn to concentrate when I'm not nervous, so I could get in position to win, then I'd be fine."

Nicklaus understood what most great athletes do—being nervous can help performance. Bill Russell, the great Boston Celtic center, wrote in his memoirs that he always felt confident the Celtics would win a big game if he threw up in the locker room before it started. A nervous stomach meant, to Russell, that he was interested and excited. If he didn't vomit, he was afraid his performance would be flat.

Being nervous produces adrenaline. Being very nervous can produce a great gush of adrenaline. That can cause the heart to pound. It can cause the hands to shake.

In a young golfer, or an older golfer who hasn't learned how to handle it, this gush of adrenaline can be devastating. He stands over a shot or a putt and feels the trembling hands and the furiously beating heart. He doesn't understand that this is simply a natural reaction to the situation. It's the way the body is wired. He begins to think, "What the heck is wrong with me?"

And that thought introduces doubt and fear, which, as we have seen, are the termites that destroy the foundation of the successful stroke. He or she may try to still the heart and hands, which makes the body stiff. He or she forgets to trust. He blames the ensuing bad shot or putt on shaking hands, not on being distracted by shaking hands.

Many players, including Val Skinner, one of the LPGA players I work with, have had to learn to handle this challenge. Under pressure, particularly on the greens, Val's hands would start to shake because of the intensity she brings to the game. She worried about this until I told her about all the critical putts that good golfers have made with shaking hands. Then she started to accept and welcome the physical symptoms of stress as a normal part of the human condition.

The successful golfer either has learned, or instinctively understands, that the pounding heart and the trembling hands are nothing to worry about. They are, at worst, another factor to be accounted for, like a following wind. They may cause an iron shot to carry 10 or 20 yards longer than it normally would. But they will not, of themselves, destroy the swing.

The successful golfer knows that rather than concern himself with stilling the hands and quieting the heart, he must focus the mind, blocking out distractions and attending to routine and strategy just as meticulously as if this were a practice round, on his home course at twilight, with no one else around. The body can and probably will stay excited. The mind must not.

Successful golfers, like Nicklaus, welcome the onset of nervous symptoms. That's why they got into competition in the first place—because winning was important to them and overcoming the emotional challenges of competitive golf gave them a great feeling of accomplishment. They play tournament golf precisely because it makes them nervous.

I sometimes tell young players that being nervous on the golf course is a little bit like being nervous the first time you make love with someone you really care about. Nearly everyone is nervous in that situation, but nerves are part of what makes the experience so exhilarating. If it didn't make you nervous, it wouldn't be so gratifying. In fact, it might be a little boring. Ask any prostitute.

So, choking is not being nervous. Choking is also not synonymous with making a bad shot in a pressure situation. Hitting a golf ball precisely is a complicated task. No human being can do it well all the time. A player can do everything right, mentally, and still miss a two-footer on the 18th hole of an important match. In golf, that simply happens sometimes. It's not necessarily due to choking. If the putt or shot is missed in spite of good thinking, the golfer simply has to accept his misfortune as part of the game, and move on.

Choking is also not the inevitable by-product of a flawed

swing, although you often hear golfers talk about trying to learn a swing that will "hold up under pressure." If a swing is good enough to repeat itself on the practice tee, it is good enough to repeat itself on the golf course, as long as the golfer's thoughts remain consistent. Swings don't hold up under pressure. People do.

And, finally, choking is not synonymous with having a flawed character. Some nasty, miserable people have triumphed under pressure. And some of the finest, most admirable human beings in the world have choked in tight situations. If you play golf long enough, you are bound to encounter some pressure situations in which you will perform at less than your best. They will help you learn how to cope with pressure, which is a skill that must be learned, and, once learned, constantly maintained.

I've already spoken of some examples of choking. We've seen how Corey Pavin let the pond on No. 16 at Augusta distract him from his target and ruin his chances at the 1986 Masters. And we've seen how Tom Kite let a missed putt cause him to abort his routine and miss a two-foot comeback putt at the U.S. Open in 1989. These are two of the toughest minds I've ever known. I could cite dozens of other examples. Raymond Floyd blew a big lead and lost the Senior PGA Championship on the final nine holes in 1994. Afterward, he told the press that he realized that under pressure, he'd been altering his setup a little, causing blocked shots.

Each of them, it should be noted, learned from the experience and went on to become a better player. Choking is not a congenital, incurable disease. It can be overcome if the golfer intelligently analyzes what went wrong in a particular situation and takes steps to correct it.

• • •

THE U.S. OPEN is perhaps our greatest laboratory for the study of performance under pressure. Golfers can quibble about whether the Masters is more lucrative or the British Open more prestigious. But no other tournament offers quite the cauldron of distractions as our Open. The sheer, overwhelming desire to win the title is itself a distraction. So is the fear of getting into contention or into the lead and then failing to capitalize. The U.S. Golf Association lets the rough grow and pinch the fairways to provide another source of doubt. It shaves the greens to make it all the more difficult to ignore any tremor in the hands. The finishing holes are invariably among the longest and most testing in golf. Not surprisingly, the history of the Open is rich in stories of golfers, many of them great golfers, who fell in the stretch with an apple stuck in their throat.

I say this knowing that I am putting myself into the position of the second-guesser in his armchair, whom I generally detest. I do not mean to besmirch anyone's character. I don't mean to gainsay the tremendous achievement of simply getting into position to blow an Open. Those who have gained such position are the warriors who dared to enter the arena, and they deserve admiration. I simply note that even the greatest players are human, human beings commit mental mistakes, and all golfers can learn from the study of those mistakes.

Arnold Palmer, who won the Open so dramatically in 1960, blew it just as dramatically in 1966 at the Olympic Club in San Francisco. Most golfers know the outlines of that story. Palmer made the turn in the final round seven strokes ahead of Billy Casper. He wound up losing the tournament to Casper in a playoff the next day.

I admire Arnold Palmer a great deal. My favorite story about him suggests how loose and trusting he was in his prime. It occurred in 1962, at the Colonial. Palmer was in a playoff with

Johnny Pott when he hit a ball into a bunker on the 9th hole. He was about to hit his recovery shot when he heard a small boy's voice, followed quickly by the sound of a mother hissing at the boy to hush. Palmer turned around and saw the two, the boy looking chagrined and the mother embarrassed. Palmer just laughed, turned back to the ball, and addressed the shot again. Just as he was about to swing, he heard another sound. This time, the mortified boy was sobbing. Palmer backed off again and again smiled at the child. Then he addressed the ball a third time. He heard a gagging sound. He turned around and saw that by this time the mother had clamped a hand over the boy's mouth.

"Hey, it's okay," Palmer said. "Don't choke him. This isn't that important."

Whereupon he blasted out of the trap and went on to win the playoff.

But four years later, Palmer was being supplanted as the best golfer in the world by Jack Nicklaus, and he desperately wanted to win the Open. He was not quite so loose.

As it happens, I have taught at clinics several times with a pro named Mike Reasor, who was Palmer's caddie during that Open. From Reasor's account, and what Palmer himself has written, it's possible to reconstruct much of what went through Palmer's mind that Sunday in San Francisco.

Palmer gave one standing instruction to his caddie that day. If his swing tempo got too fast, he wanted Reasor to tell him. Reasor was himself a top-flight golfer, a member of the Brigham Young University team. And he noticed on the 7th hole of the final round that Palmer's tempo was quickening. But, he reasoned, who was he to correct the best player in golf, a man leading the Open by seven strokes? Reasor kept his counsel for the time being.

Palmer has written that as he stood on the 10th tee, he was so confident of victory that he stopped thinking about the shot immediately ahead of him and started thinking about breaking the Open scoring record of 276, set by Ben Hogan in 1948. Palmer already held the British Open scoring record. The thought of holding both records simultaneously enchanted him. Distracted by that thought, he lost a stroke to Casper on No. 10.

At No. 11, he hit his tee shot into the right rough. Reasor was trailing eight or ten paces behind Palmer as they set off from the 11th tee. He had noticed that the swing was getting even quicker. He decided to tell Palmer.

"I called out, 'Arnold,' and he stopped and looked around," Reasor recalled. "I told him his swing had gotten way faster. He made an attempt thereafter to gear it down, but it was difficult. Trying to slow it down took away his free flow and put tension in the swing."

Palmer had already committed, in retrospect, two of the common mental mistakes a golfer makes under pressure. He had let his thoughts drift into the future. He had started to dwell on the score he was shooting and the Open record. Then, he compounded the error by introducing a new, mechanical thought, about swing tempo. As I've mentioned, tempo is one of the least harmful swing thoughts a golfer can have. But introducing such a thought at an advanced stage of a critical round is not the same as starting with it on the first tee. Fear of a quick backswing often leads to a tentative forward swing. In Palmer's case it probably would have been better to continue to play with no swing thought at all, because, as Reasor noticed, trying to slow the swing down did more harm than good. Palmer managed to par No. 11, but Casper birdied No. 13. The lead was down to five.

Then Palmer made the third mistake commonly committed

by golfers under pressure. He started trying to be too bold. The 15th hole at Olympic is a short, heavily bunkered par three, and the USGA had chosen a sucker pin position, just beyond a deep trap. Palmer went for the pin, fell short of the green by inches, and wound up in the sand. He bogeyed the hole. Casper hit to the center of the green, sank the putt, and cut the lead to three.

No. 16 at Olympic is a long par five, playing 604 yards that day. Obviously, at that length, it was unreachable in two shots. The conservative strategy would have been to play a couple of 1-irons down the fairway, then hit a wedge to the green. But Palmer hated playing conservatively. He had used his driver in each of the three previous rounds from the 16th tee.

As he stood there, waiting for Casper to hit, Palmer mulled over his strategy. He thought about a 1-iron. But then he decided that he couldn't do that, that Arnold Palmer would look silly playing safe with a 1-iron, trying to protect a three-stroke lead with three holes to play. So he took out his driver and duck-hooked the ball into the trees and rough.

His ball was buried in thick, wiry grass. But Palmer was still intent on boldness.

"Can I get a 3-iron on the ball?" he asked Reasor.

Reasor thought the lie was too difficult for a 3-iron, that it called for a much more lofted club. But he was afraid to tell Palmer that.

"Only with a perfect swing," Reasor said.

Palmer decided that if a perfect swing was required, he would simply have to produce a perfect swing. He tried the 3-iron. But he barely got the club on the ball, moving it only 40 or 50 yards, still in the rough. He hit a 9-iron into the fairway, then a 3-wood to a greenside bunker. He managed to get up and down for a bogey. Casper, meanwhile, played three safe shots to the green and sank a putt for a birdie. The lead was down to one stroke.

It evaporated completely on the 17th, when Palmer missed the green, played a good recovery, but missed a five-footer for par.

Would the Open have ended differently if Palmer had played conservatively? It's impossible to tell. Mike Reasor points out that the swing Palmer made on the disastrous tee shot at No. 16 would have produced a disastrous shot with a 1-iron as well. But we will never know if he would have made that swing with a 1-iron. There are no hard and fast rules for strategy and tactics.

But it's instructive to compare what Palmer did with what Jack Nicklaus did in a roughly similar Open situation a year later, at Baltusrol.

Palmer and Nicklaus made up the final twosome of the tournament, and as they came to the 18th hole, Nicklaus was four strokes ahead. Not only that, but a birdie would break Hogan's record of 276.

The 18th at Baltusrol is a 542-yard par five, dogleg left, lined with trees, reachable with two good shots. A creek cuts across the fairway about 400 yards from the tee. Nicklaus, of course, wanted the record. But he wanted even more to make sure that he won the tournament.

Nicklaus pulled out his 1-iron.

As it happened, he made a bad swing, much as Palmer had done on the 16th tee at Olympic the year before. He sliced the ball into the rough. He could have tried the heroic shot there. But he played an 8-iron, expecting to lay up short of the creek. He mishit it and moved the ball only about 100 yards, but into the fairway. Palmer, meanwhile, played his second shot just off the green.

At that point, Nicklaus hit one of the great shots of his career, a 235-yard 1-iron to the green. He sank the putt and got the record anyway.

The difference between what Nicklaus did in 1967 and what Palmer did in 1966 is subtle but instructive. Both made some bad shots under pressure. But Nicklaus was playing more conservatively, more within himself. He accepted the fact that once he put the ball into the Open rough from the tee, he would have to play a lofted club. His bad swings, as a result, got him into a little less trouble. And when the time came to make a truly difficult shot, he was in a much stronger, calmer mental state. His success reflected it.

A WEEKEND PLAYER can only imagine what it must be like to stand in Palmer's shoes, trying to hang on to a dwindling lead in the U.S. Open. But the lessons of Palmer's collapse are just as applicable to coping with the pressures of a two-dollar Nassau or the final holes of a club tournament.

First, stay in the present and keep your mind sharply focused on the shot immediately in front of you.

Don't, as Palmer did when he started thinking of the Open scoring record, let extraneous thoughts distract you. If you're ahead, don't start calculating whom you'll play in the next round, or what kind of beer you'll order with the two dollars. If you're behind, don't start thinking about losing the match or about how well your opponent played the last few holes.

Second, avoid mechanical thoughts, such as the tempo thought Palmer allowed into his mind. Instead, strive to become looser, freer and more confident. You should want to feel that you trust your swing more on the 18th tee than you did on the 1st.

Third, stick to your routine and to your game plan.

You set them up to give you a chance to post your lowest possible number by having a conservative stragety and a cocky, aggressive swing. If you make some mistakes and fall behind early, there's no reason to try to make up the deficit with bold, risky strategy, like Palmer's 3-iron out of the rough on No. 16. Don't start firing at tight pins where you'd planned to aim for the middle of the green. Don't hit a driver from a tee where you planned to hit an iron. You're far more likely to come back by playing steadily and well and giving your opponent a chance to make some mistakes of his own.

NERVE-WRACKING DISTRACTIONS are not, of course, peculiar to the U.S. Open. They can occur on any course at any time, even in a casual round.

Some golfers get upset when play slows down in front of them. It's often hard not to. But if you dwell on it, you can convince yourself that the delays are going to throw off your rhythm and ruin your round. You may even come up against a player who will deliberately agree with you that the slow play is aggravating and damaging and take quiet delight in destroying your composure.

The only effective response to bottlenecks on the course is a decision that they will not bother you. You can even try to enjoy the languor of it. If you have to wait, keep walking around to make sure that the body stays active and warm. If you must sit, be certain that a few minutes before your turn to hit finally comes around, you stand up, stretch a little, walk around, and get the body limber again. Then go through your routine once or twice in your mind. Get yourself focused back on golf.

Even if there are no undue delays, much of the time in a

round of golf will be consumed by things other than shotmaking
—walking to your ball and watching your partners play theirs. I
recommend getting your mind off of golf between shots. It's
easier for most people to concentrate totally for a minute or so
at a time, as they execute their shotmaking routines. Trying to
stay that focused between shots can be too taxing. Some players,
like Lee Trevino and Fuzzy Zoeller, chat constantly between
shots as a way of staying loose. Brad Faxon will sometimes step
behind the gallery ropes to chat with friends who are following
him around.

If you or your partners don't want to talk, try something else.
Look at the birds or trees or weeds. Jack Nicklaus used to scan
the gallery for pretty girls and joke about setting up his caddie,
Angelo Argea, on dates with them.

Of course, Zoeller, Trevino, Faxon and Nicklaus all switch
their attention completely to the task at hand once it's time to
play a shot.

If there's a rain delay, it's even more essential to unwind
and distance yourself from golf. Read a book. Change clothes.
When the rain stops, make up your mind that the delay is
going to help you. Warm back up by going through your routine
on a few practice swings, simulating a real shot as closely as
possible.

Finally, the play of your opponents can be a nervous distraction. Many a player has been cruising along in a match until his
opponent suddenly and unexpectedly sinks a long chip or
comes out of the woods to make par. Surprised, he loses his
focus, starts to feel pressured, and fouls up his own game.

A golfer should always assume that his opponent will hit the
best possible shot. Then, if it happens, he'll be prepared to cope
with it. I saw a great example of this some years back at the
Tournament Players' Championship. Tom Kite and Chip Beck

were leading the tournament going into the final round, and they formed the final twosome.

Chip started out horribly, making four bogeys on the front side and shooting 40. Tom seemed to have a comfortable lead. But Tom did not assume that Chip would keep playing that badly, or even that he would play the back nine in par figures. Instead, he assumed that Chip would get as hot on the back side as he had been cold on the front. And Chip did, shooting 31. Tom, however, was ready for that kind of charge. He stuck to his game plan, and he held Chip off until the final hole. There, Tom teed off with a two-stroke lead.

They both reached the green in regulation figures. Tom was 50 feet and two tiers of green away. Chip had a tricky, downhill putt of 25 feet.

Immediately, Tom told me later, he assumed Chip would make that putt, difficult though it was. He rolled his first putt to about five feet.

Then, sure enough, Chip made his birdie putt.

If Chip's putt had surprised or unnerved Tom, his next putt would have suddenly become much harder. But because Tom had prepared himself mentally, his emotional state did not change when Chip's ball disappeared into the hole. Things were still going as he had planned. He was still in control.

And he holed his par putt and won the tournament.

19.

When the Scoreboard

Looks at You

ONE OF THE most common mental errors committed by golfers under pressure is letting the score distract them from what they ought to be thinking about.

No one paid more dearly for this mistake than Sam Snead in the U.S. Open of 1939 at Spring Mill, outside Philadelphia. Snead set the Open pace that year with rounds of 68, 71 and 73. As he stood on the 17th tee in the final round, he added up his own total. He knew that par on the final two holes would give him a 69 for 281, tying the Open record Ralph Guldahl had set two years earlier.

In those days, tournament courses had no leaderboards. Nor were the leaders always paired in the final rounds. News of other players' scores flitted around the course by word of mouth, and the news was not always accurate. Byron Nelson, Snead's closest pursuer, had come in at 284. Snead erroneously thought, however, that Nelson had finished a stroke or two better than that.

Not knowing he had a 3-shot lead, he decided to go all out on 17 and hit a 300-yard drive. But his second shot was in the rough, and his chip was short. He bogeyed the hole.

Walking to the par-five 18th, thinking that he had probably fallen into a tie with Nelson, Snead completely lost his natural serenity. He had nervous physical symptoms; his teeth, he recalled later, were chattering. The gallery distracted him. The rush of people coming over to 18 from 17 forced him to wait. He started thinking about the money he stood to blow. He thought about the annoying gallery. He thought about avoiding humiliation. He thought he needed a birdie to win. He thought, in short, about everything but the right way to play No. 18.

Half a century later, Snead still was angry with the gallery, still wondered why no one told him that the score to beat was 284, not 282 or 283. He needed only a bogey to win the Open. But the fact of the matter is that he himself let extraneous thoughts dominate his mind. He let the score distract him. He let the gallery distract him. He did not focus intently on a game plan for No. 18, take each shot as it came and stick with his routine.

Trying to hit another huge drive, he hooked the ball into the deep Open rough. Still thinking he needed a birdie, he tried to hit a 2-wood out of the rough, rather than taking a midiron. He hit, in other words, the shot he thought he should hit rather than the shot he knew he could hit. He topped it.

The ball came to rest in a fairway trap, a hundred yards from the green, half-buried. Snead was desperate to reach the green. He took an 8-iron, rather than a sand wedge. The ball hit the lip. His fourth shot found a greenside trap. He blasted out and, thoroughly discombobulated, three-putted, for a total of eight strokes. He had given the Open away, and after that he never would win one.

Would he have won if he had known the correct score? Perhaps. If thinking about the score accurately can be a dangerous distraction, thinking about a false score is even worse.

But he almost certainly would have won if he had not paid attention to the score. Once he started thinking about it, he introduced a host of distracting thoughts. He let the score, rather than common sense, dictate club selection and strategy. Sitting in the rough after his tee shot at No. 18, Snead was 260 yards from the green. He could have hit a 7-iron and a wedge, leaving himself a putt for the birdie he thought he needed. Instead, he tried for the shot that was too bold, too difficult, and in the end disastrous.

Pressure frequently doesn't do nearly as much damage to a golfer's swing as it does to his course management.

IN FOCUSING so much of his thinking on his own score and those of the other players, Snead did something I advise golfers to avoid, whether they're in the final round of the Open or just a friendly round.

The minute you start thinking, "If I shoot bogey for the last three holes I'll break 90," or "if I shoot par for the next two holes I'll win the Open," you get ahead of yourself. Your thoughts leave the present. You start worrying too much about fouling things up. You get careful. You get tight. You start steering the ball instead of getting looser and cockier. You play the golfing equivalent of pro football's prevent defense. And disaster often strikes, whether your goal is to break 90 or win the Open.

High-handicappers as a rule pay much closer attention to

their scores than pros do. They can't wait to write down the number after every hole. They're always adding up their strokes and using the number as a way of evaluating how they're doing. If they start to approach a goal, like breaking 90, they're instantly aware of what they have to do on the remaining holes to reach it. It's one of the reasons they're high-handicappers. They make it much harder on themselves.

Professionals, when they're playing at home, rarely use a scorecard. When the round is over, they recollect each hole, add up the strokes and determine their score. That's what the average player should do.

I know it's not easy. Golfers have ingrained the habit of writing down the score after every hole, adding it up after 9, and projecting the total over 18. Playing partners often will do this for them if they don't. If there are bets on the match, that adds to the tendency to keep constant track of the score.

I can only say that you'll shoot a lower score, on average, if you keep your mind in the present and take it one shot at a time.

For modern professionals, the task is harder because there are leaderboards everywhere on the courses they play, and they have to make a conscious decision not to let them distract them.

Jack Nicklaus was excellent at this. Angelo Argea, his longtime caddie, wrote that as a rule, Nicklaus did not want to know how the field was faring and rarely looked at a leaderboard. Once, Argea said, Nicklaus started a final round leading a tournament by several strokes. He ordered Argea not to tell him what the leaderboards said. The caddie stayed mum. But on the 16th tee, Nicklaus suddenly turned to Argea and demanded to know where he stood.

"You're nine strokes ahead," Argea told him.

Nicklaus double-bogeyed the hole.

There are players, of course, who do keep an eye on the leaderboard and want to know where they stand, particularly in the final holes of a tournament. Nick Price is one of them. They like the challenge of knowing the entire situation and dealing with it. If they are successful players, though, you can be sure that they take the score information in and then refocus their attention entirely on the next shot. For most players, it's easier, in my opinion, to pay no attention to the score.

VAL SKINNER TELLS me she has won several tournaments without knowing, until she holed her last putt, that she had won. She's won tournaments knowing, from the way the crowd applauded her, that she had the lead, but not knowing by how many strokes. She makes a deliberate effort to avoid looking at leaderboards. She counts on her caddie to tell her, on the final few holes, if there's anything critical she needs to know about the standings. This means, for instance, that if she's a stroke out of the lead on a par-five final hole, she wants to know. It could affect her decision on whether to lay up or try to reach the green in two. Otherwise, she understands that there is nothing she can do to affect her opponents' scores. She maximizes her chances to win by refusing to think about anything but her own routine and her own game plan.

At the Atlanta Women's Championship in 1994, at Eagle's Landing, Val started the final round two strokes behind Liselotte Neumann. Neumann tripled-bogeyed the first hole, and Val, in the final threesome with her, knew she was close to the lead, if not leading. She decided to pretend, however, that someone in the group in front of them had the lead. She refused to look at a leaderboard. She stuck to her game plan. She played a round that verged on brilliance. Neumann, however, steadied herself and kept pace with Val.

On the 17th, a dogleg par four, Val hit her drive a little left of her target, into a bunker. She tried to hit too much club out of the bunker, and barely got on the green in three. She had a 20-foot putt for par. Neumann had a 3-foot putt for par.

An enormous leaderboard stood behind the green. Val tried to keep her eyes from focusing it, but suddenly, she could not. The numbers and letters, as if of their own volition, pulled into sharp clarity.

The board said she was leading Neumann by one stroke.

The information did not help her concentration as she stood over the 20-footer. It was a slippery, downhill putt with perhaps an 8-foot break. Once she knew that missing it could cost her the tournament, it started to look even slipperier, as if she were trying to bank the ball off a green, marble cliff.

She left her putt 8 feet short.

Fortunately, at that point, all the work Val had been doing to learn to control her thoughts and discipline her mind paid off. She confronted the challenge to set aside all of the distractions. She forgot the standings. And she made her 8-footer.

Then Neumann missed her 3-footer.

The scoreboard, in effect, had given Val a false picture. She had assumed that Neumann would make her 3-foot par putt and tie for the lead if she missed her own par putt. It was a false assumption. But that false assumption, plus the information from the leaderboard, made her own par putt harder than it needed to be and nearly cost her the tournament.

Of course, it's very difficult to block out the score.

"Doc," Val told me later, "I didn't want to look at that leaderboard. But it was like that leaderboard was looking at me."

20.

Competitors

SOME MONTHS AFTER I started working with Tom Kite in 1984, he started recommending me to other golfers on the tour. One of them got to wondering.

"Wait a minute," he said to Tom. "If this guy Rotella helps you, why do you want him to help us? We're your competitors."

"The way I see it," Tom replied, "there's more than enough money out here for all of us. You guys are going to help me get better. And I'm going to help you get better. We're all going to help each other have fun seeing how good we can get."

Tom had the ideal attitude toward competition and his fellow competitors.

He recognized that the other people on the golf course are not the real opposition that a golfer faces.

The first opponent is the game itself. The course, the club

and the ball are all idiosyncratic and unpredictable foes, and they will humble the best golfer more than occasionally.

The second opponent is the golfer himself. Can he discipline his mind to produce the best score his body is capable of?

Only after those two foes have been confronted do the other people on the course come into the picture.

The best athletes realize that if they win the battle with themselves, they have done all they can do. The golfer who can look back on a tournament that he lost and say, "I played as well as I could. I had my mind where it was supposed to be on every shot," will be satisfied and happy.

This is true in all sports. When I worked with professional baseball pitcher Greg Maddux I suggested he approach pitching in much the same way a golfer approaches a golf course. He needed a plan for facing each hitter. He needed a target for each pitch, and a velocity. If he delivered a pitch precisely as he wanted to, he should be satisfied. If Bobby Bonds then hit the ball out of the park, Greg did not consider himself a failure.

Big-league hitters could do that. That's why they were in the big leagues. Testing himself against the best, Maddux would not get everyone out. But testing himself against the best would help him find out just how good he could be.

The best golfers have much the same attitude. Their primary concern is performing as well as they can, or as close to their potential as they can get. If they do that, and lose, they shrug and go on. They know that if they keep performing as well as they can, the wins will come. And they do.

That's why a player like Tom Kite can want to help his competitors play better. He realizes that if they improve their games, it will motivate him to do what it takes to get better. He will move closer to finding out how well he can play.

Most of the touring players I work with come to me because

another player advised them to do so. Typically, two friends will sit down for dinner during a tournament, and one will ask the second why he or she seems to be playing better. This happened a lot in 1993 and 1994 to Nick Price, for obvious reasons. Nick would always be happy to share with players how he had learned to discipline and focus his mind on the golf course. And if they wanted to know more, he gave them my number.

The point is that it never occurred to Nick not to want his competitors to get better. Nor would it occur to any of the players I work with.

So it distresses me when I run into players, usually lesser players, who think it's smart to use gamesmanship to throw off opponents in competitive tournaments. They're always pointing out water hazards or swing flaws.

Such players must be treated as unfortunate distractions, like a slow foursome in front or the greenskeeper's lawn mower roaring to life across a fairway. A golfer simply has to put them out of his mind, get on with his routine, and tend to his business.

Gamesmanship experts hurt themselves. If they are touring players, they will soon be subtly or not so subtly warned to cut it out. If they fail to heed the warning, they will be shunned. The tour, no matter how much money they make, will be a lonely and unhappy place for them.

If they are amateurs, they risk foregoing one of the great joys of the game, friendships with fellow players.

So I advise players at all levels to cherish their competitors. It's better for their games. It's better for them.

Never decide that you can't stand another golfer, because you might find yourself paired with that golfer for the most important round of your life.

On the other hand, a golfer can't let admiration for a competi-

tor intimidate him. A golfer has to choose someone to believe
in. It had better be himself.

I work occasionally with some of the players on the Senior
Tour, like Larry Laoretti, who spent their twenties, thirties and
forties working as club pros and watching players like Jack
Nicklaus and Lee Trevino on television. Nicklaus, in particular,
was their ideal. Now, they have to be prepared to face a Nicklaus
or a Trevino over the final holes of a tournament.

I tell them that if they want to keep Nicklaus on a pedestal, if
they want to look at him as a hero, they ought to buy a ticket
and watch the tournament instead of entering it. If they want to
step onto the golf course with him, they have to believe they
can beat him.

I sometimes tell golfers a story about a basketball player I
worked with at Virginia named Olden Polyniece, who is pres-
ently in his ninth year of playing in the National Basketball
Association. He had one of the best minds for sports I've ever
encountered.

In 1984, Olden's first year, the basketball team got off to a
mediocre start, breaking even in its first few games. The coaching staff decided to put Olden in the starting lineup, at center.
His first game would be against North Carolina, in Chapel Hill.
The Tar Heels had a fair team that year. It included Michael
Jordan, James Worthy and Sam Perkins. They were undefeated
and ranked first in all the polls.

Olden learned that he would be starting against them at the
team's weekly Sunday night dinner in the back room of a local
restaurant. After the players left, Olden walked back into the
room, where the coaches and I were still sitting and talking.
Olden stepped up to me and said, "Hey, Doc, I've got a question.
How am I supposed to believe in myself if this is my first start
ever, and we're going up against the No. 1 team on its home

court, and we're playing against guys I loved to watch on television when I was in high school?"

I was impressed with the candor of Olden's question. He didn't care that the coaches were listening. All he knew was that he had to get ready to play Jordan, Perkins and Worthy.

"You've got to go in there with the attitude that you're better than they are until they prove otherwise, rather than the attitude that they're better than you are until you prove otherwise," I told him. "Put the burden of proof on them."

"That's a good idea," Olden said.

He went down to Chapel Hill and played a beautiful game. He had something like 15 points and 18 rebounds. The team lost by a point at the buzzer. Then, with its confidence buoyed, it went on to record a string of upsets in the NCAA tournament and reach the Final Four. Olden may not have been quite good enough that night to lead his team to a victory but he had begun to demonstrate an attitude that would assure him of future success.

Golf is much the same. Great players lose more tournaments than they win because players with just a bit less talent got more out of their talent in a particular week. Certainly, Nicklaus at twenty-five was better than Larry Laoretti at twenty-five. But that doesn't necessarily mean Nicklaus will be better at fifty-five. Some golfers progress. Some regress. Some get hungrier and double their commitment. Some lose their hunger, develop other interests, or develop other priorities. The USGA Junior champion rarely goes on to become the Open champion.

And what someone did to you in last year's club championship—or what you did to him—has nothing to do with what happens if you meet in this year's tournament.

21.

....

Practicing to Improve

....
....
....

THE GOOD PLAYERS I work with don't have to be told to practice. Most of them have grown up believing that hard work and dedication pay off in success. When something goes wrong with their games, their first instinct is to head for the practice area. Then they start working on fixing their problems.

This kind of attitude has won them praise all of their lives. Americans believe in the work ethic. They believe that practice makes perfect, and the best players are the ones who practice the most.

So good golfers grow up thinking that time spent on practice is automatically time well spent. And that attitude takes them a fairly long way. If they have enough talent, it can make them scratch golfers. It can win them college scholarships.

But it rarely can take them to the next level, the level required to win on the PGA Tour. To do that, a lot of them have to learn to back off a little, to stop investing all their time and energy in the fruitless pursuit of mechanical perfection. They need to learn to practice in a different way.

In golf, working hard does not guarantee success. It can even make things worse. Doing the wrong things in practice can ruin your golfing mind.

To improve, you must practice. But the quality of your practice is more important than the quantity.

Go to any practice tee or driving range and watch the way most golfers hit balls.

Many of them don't even bother to select a target before they hit a ball. They would laugh if you suggested that they practice shooting a basketball without using a basket. But they bash golf ball after golf ball into the ether, blithely unconcerned with hitting a target. When they get onto a course, focusing on a target is a new experience for them.

Others spend an entire practice session trying to break the swing down into its component parts and work on one or more of those parts. They may focus on their swing planes, or their hip turns, or their right elbows. But their practice sessions are entirely mechanical. When they get onto a course, they tend to think mechanically.

To understand how to practice you must first understand that there are two states of mind in practice—the training mentality and the trusting mentality.

In the training mentality, a golfer evaluates his shots critically and analytically. In the trusting mentality, the golfer simply accepts them.

In the training mentality, the golfer tries to make things happen. In the trusting mentality, the golfer lets things happen.

The training mentality is very thoughtful. The trusting mentality feels like reckless abandon.

The training mentality is impatient. The trusting mentality is patient.

In the training mentality, a player may just rake ball after ball into position, working on something mechanical. In the trusting mentality, he goes through his shotmaking routine with every ball he hits.

This distinction is not a matter of good versus bad. Both the training mentality and the trusting mentality have their places in a golfer's practice sessions.

The training mentality is essential for incorporating swing changes and for working on the swing fundamentals. Even at the top levels of the game, players constantly work on maintaining their setup and preshot fundamentals as well as basic swing mechanics. The best athletes in the world always spend a portion of their practice time in the training mentality.

One of the things that separates a pro like Tom Kite from the average golfer is that Tom doesn't wait until his game goes sour to try to remedy things. As soon as he detects the slightest problem with any of the fundamental shots, with setup and routine, or with his mental game, Tom drops whatever else he's doing and heads to the practice area to fix it. That's one reason he's such a consistent money winner. When he does this, he's immersed in the training mentality.

Professionals, as they practice in the training mentality, evaluate themselves harshly. An iron shot may go precisely where they aimed it, but if the trajectory is not what they wanted, they will pick apart the swing and remain dissatisfied until the ball flies to the target with the exact arc and curve they want.

BUT THE TRUSTING mentality is essential for getting ready to play competitively. If you want to be able to trust your swing on the golf course, you have to spend time doing it on the practice tee. Human beings are creatures of habit. They cannot, as a general rule, spend all of their practice time in the training mentality and then switch to the trusting mentality for competition. Under pressure, an athlete's dominant habit will emerge. An athlete who spends most of his practice time in the training mentality will generally fall into the training mentality when he least wants to, when the pressure is greatest. He will start thinking analytically, judgmentally and mechanically. He will not be able to trust his swing and let it go.

The dominant habit is the one an athlete practices most. Therefore:

You must spend at least 60 percent of your practice time in the trusting mentality.

This means, in general, that if you hit a hundred balls in a practice session, at least sixty should be hit in the trusting mentality. This isn't easy, because it requires that you shut your mind down except for thoughts of target and routine. The second an imperfect shot leaves your clubface, you will confront the temptation to evaluate and criticize the swing that produced the imperfect shot, to rake another ball up, and to try to fix the problem. If you can't learn to resist this temptation, your practice time will be less productive than it should be and you will never be as good as you can be.

The 60 percent rule is a general guideline. There should be some practice sessions where you spend more time in the training mentality and others where you spend nearly all your time in the trusting mentality.

You may spend more time in the training mentality at the beginning of the season, when you're trying to restore the mechanics and rhythm that tend to slip away during the winter.

You may spend more time in the training mentality when you're trying to fix a problem that has cropped up in your game.

Conversely, the closer a player gets to competition, the more practice time he must spend in the trusting mentality. A player preparing for a tournament should hit 70 to 90 percent of his practice shots in the trusting mentality in the last days before the competition begins. He needs to accustom the mind to the style of thinking that works on the golf course—to thoughts of target, of routine, of acceptance.

This is particularly true of the warm-up period just before a round. This is preparation for competition, when trusting works. At this stage, a player ought to strive to hit all of his shots in the trusting mentality. If he lets himself revert to the training mentality and starts trying to fix swing mechanics, it will be very difficult to get back into the trusting mentality on the first tee. For a competitive round, a player should get to the course at least an hour ahead of time so he can spend his warm-up period steeped in patience and trust. This is not a time to be rushing from practice tee to putting green to first tee, stuffing a candy bar into your mouth on the fly.

While no good pro that I know of tries to fix his swing while he's warming up before a round, a lot of them do work on their mechanics after a round, trying to fix flaws that they noticed during that day's play. If a player wants to do this, I let him. It certainly is better for him than going back to the hotel and brooding about the mistakes. I hope he leaves the practice area with his confidence restored, ready to trust his swing the next day.

But Tom Watson told me that he made the big breakthrough in his career after he learned to stop working on his mistakes after a round. Suppose he'd played a round where he mishit a couple of wedges. Earlier in his career, he might work for an hour and a half on wedges. But the next day, he'd find that he was concentrating so much on wedges that some other facet of his game suffered. So he changed his postround practice habits. He started working for forty minutes on a little bit of everything, not just on the clubs and shots that had been less than perfect that day. He realized that a single day's results, no matter how bad, never justified trying to overhaul his swing mechanics in the middle of a tournament.

Regardless of how close a player is to competition, I'm not a great believer in hitting bucket after bucket with the full swing just for the sake of hitting them. It's an easy way to develop bad habits.

An amateur, particularly, would be far better off hitting a couple of dozen balls three times a week, going through his routine on every ball, picking out a target, and trusting. He would at least be on his way to ingraining mental discipline and getting the best score out of the swing he has.

And any player, whether touring pro or weekend duffer, should spend the majority of his practice time on the short game, on shots of 120 yards and less.

I'd begin by going to a practice green and starting on the fringe. I recommend that good players practice chips every day until they sink two. This does two things. First, it forces them to think about holing chips rather than just getting them on the green in the direction of the hole. And it boosts their confidence. It's amazing how sinking a couple of chips every day can persuade a player that he has a great short game.

Weekend players may not be able to practice long enough to sink two chips. Darkness or divorce proceedings would intervene. They can still drop a dozen balls at various spots around the green and see how many they can get up and down, using their full routines with every shot.

The weekend player ought to make sure he has a few fundamental short shots in his arsenal. One would be the chip from the edge of the green. The second would be the flop shot from a little farther off the putting surface. And the third would be a sand explosion that got up in the air, traveled about 15 or 20 feet, and could be relied on to get out of any greenside bunker.

Once he has practiced those shots, he should move to the practice tee and start working at shots from 40 to 120 yards. Hit lots of different shots: pitch-and-runs, knockdowns, different trajectories. Always have a small target. This will develop feel and touch.

The short shots around the green save pars. The longer wedge shots, from 120 yards to about 40 yards, make birdies. Players can't practice them too much.

I like to see players competing at short-game drills. Bet a nickel, a beer or a soda. Drop balls at varying distances, into varying lies. Award five points for holing a shot and three for hitting it within tap-in distance. It introduces competitive pressure, it sharpens the instinct to hit the target, and it makes practice fun.

A player ought to spend, as a general rule, no more than 30 percent of his practice time on the full swing. And of this time, the bulk should be spent with the club—anything from a driver to a 3-iron—that he uses when he absolutely has to put the ball into the fairway. How much time should be reserved for the long irons and midirons? Almost none, especially if practice time is limited.

I also don't believe a golfer should spend hours practicing

putts. Good putting is primarily a function of attitude and routine. Once a player masters those two, he really doesn't need to hit a lot of practice putts. Bobby Locke didn't. Ben Crenshaw doesn't.

But there are several practice drills I find quite useful in putting.

I encourage players I work with to use a chalk line. This is a device that uses a reel of chalked string to lay down a line on a flat section of green, from the hole to the ball. A lot of players find that this helps them make putt after putt. The image tends to become so vivid that they can then go out on the golf course and see the line much more easily.

Often I ask a player to go to the practice green with a ball and place it 8 to 12 feet from the hole. I ask him to take nine putts and to try a little bit *less* with each putt, until he finds just the right amount of intensity. When he's found it, I ask him to try to maintain that level for five putts.

I also ask players to go to the practice green and putt to the fringe from all possible distances, merely looking at the fringe and reacting to it with each stroke. The idea is get to the edge of the green without going into the fringe. This helps players develop a feel for pace, which is the key to long putts. This drill avoids the pitfall of putting at a hole from long distances, which is that a golfer is bound to miss most of these attempts, eroding his confidence.

If a player wants to practice his putting mechanics, I suggest that he do it without a ball, indoors. Tie a piece of string, about six inches off the floor, to a couple of chairs. Step up until your eyes are over the string and the alignment line on your putter is underneath and parallel to the string. Then practice your putting stroke, trying to make the line on the putter blade stay parallel to the string. Think about the mechanical ideas you want to work on. But don't think about mechanics when you're actually putting a golf ball. Then you want to think only of the target.

Regardless of what putting drills a golfer uses, he should be certain, if he uses a ball and a cup, that he practices making putts. Practicing misses does no good. Yet I see lots of players standing 15 feet from the cup, missing nine out of ten practice putts. They may tell me that they don't get bothered by practice misses, that they're only putting for mechanics and pace, but their eyes see the misses and their minds record them.

So, work hard on putts from two to four feet. Make putt after putt. I sometimes ask players to make twenty-five in a row from that distance.

This is particularly important in the preround practice period. Putt to the fringe from every distance and angle until you are confident you can judge the pace of any putt you will encounter on the course. Then sink a few from short range, using your full putting routine.

Then go on to your long shots. If you find, as you warm up with longer shots, that you're hitting the ball well, you must believe that this is the way you will hit the ball once the round begins. If, on the other hand, you can't find your clubface as you warm up, you must believe that you're saving your good shots for the golf course.

Years ago, when I broached this idea to a group of touring players, Roger Maltbie raised his hand and said, "Wait a minute, Doc. You can't have it both ways. Either you play like you warm up or you don't."

I answered by asking what the goal was. The goal was to play well. That being the case, you have to have it both ways.

This is what Tom Kite did recently when he set the scoring record in the Bob Hope tournament out in Palm Springs. As he

204 • GOLF IS NOT A GAME OF PERFECT

warmed up for the final round, he couldn't hit the ball very well at all, at least not by his standards. He reacted by making up his mind that his play on the course would be just the opposite of his play on the practice tee.

He had to do this. Otherwise, as I said to Roger Maltbie, his best option would have been to drop out of the tournament and go home.

YOU WILL CERTAINLY spend more time in the training mentality if you're taking lessons and trying to make changes in the way you swing. No one knows how long it takes an individual to learn a new physical technique—say, a new backswing plane—well enough so that it becomes a habit that repeats itself when he swings without thinking of mechanics. It depends in part on how ingrained the old habit was. It depends in part on how well the individual practices. Does he make the new move correctly each time he practices it? Certainly, if he hits every practice ball with a teacher present, giving him accurate feedback, he will incorporate the improvement that much faster.

Ideally, if you were trying to make a change in your swing, you would stop playing golf for a few weeks while you worked on the practice tee in the training mentality. You would know you had mastered the change when you could switch to the trusting mentality and count on the new swing to repeat itself reasonably well. Then you'd be ready to go back out on the course and play.

I know that this may be more than a lot of amateurs are prepared to do. They want to improve their swings, but they also want to play their regular Sunday morning matches with their friends. Their habit is to take sporadic lessons. Since they are sporadic, their pro may figure he's only got one hour to convey everything these pupils need to know. He overloads them with fixes for all the flaws in their swings.

The golfers then try to incorporate all those changes as they play. Almost inevitably, their scores initially go up, because they are out on the course thinking about their mechanics, particularly about the changes the pro has suggested. After a week or two of frustration, they often react by consciously or unconsciously forgetting about the new techniques and going back to what they have always done. Their scores drop back to their normal range, because they begin to trust their swings again. But they wind up roughly where they started. They make no progress.

A good golfer seeks help differently. David Frost, who never took a lesson until he was a scratch golfer, tells me that he mentally filters what he hears from any teacher he consults. "When I take a lesson," he says, "my teacher can say eight or ten things to me, and I'll be saying to myself, 'Nope. Nope. That's not it. Nope.' But one of those eight or ten things will appeal to me. I'll know it will help, and I'll incorporate it and play better."

Players without Frosty's knowledge of his own swing would be smart to let their pros know that they want to commit themselves to a long-term plan of regular lessons and improvement. The pro, if he's good, would respond by giving this kind of pupil no more than one change per lesson and one swing thought to help incorporate that change. The player would use that swing thought—but only on shots of more than 120 yards—until the new habit was ingrained. He would spend at least twelve hours on the practice range, working on the new move, before taking the next lesson. Then he would go on to the next change and a new swing thought. Over a year's time, any player would improve under this regimen. And eventually, he or she would acquire a fundamentally sound swing and could play without swing thoughts.

The particular swing mechanics a pro teaches matter much less than the confidence he or she engenders in the pupils. If you encounter a professional who conveys the idea that you don't have the talent to play well, drop him or her. You have to expect some awkwardness for a while as you try to master new movements. But if, after six months or so, you still feel awkward and still lack confidence, it may be time to consider switching teachers. Find a teacher who believes in you, who encourages and supports you, who makes certain you leave the lesson tee feeling better about your game than you did when you arrived.

In my experience, a model for all golf teachers is Bob Toski. He's a great player. He's also a trick-shot artist, a singer, a dancer and a raconteur. That's not why he's a great teacher. He's a great teacher because he believes in his students and will do whatever he has to do to help them improve.

I first met Bob when I started working with the staff of the week-long *Golf Digest* schools, adding a day or two of talks on the mental side of the game to the instruction on the swing that Toski and his colleagues gave. At one of the first of these collaborations, I arrived at about 3 A.M. on Thursday morning. As I walked wearily into my hotel room, I heard a voice from the next room:

"Rotella, get in here!"

It was Bob. He was sitting up in his king-sized bed, looking like a little pea against the pillows.

"I've been waiting for you. Sit down," he said. "We've got a seventy-eight-year-old lady with a thirty-five handicap here this week. I've been trying everything with her, and I can't get her to swing inside to out and draw the ball. Give me some ideas.

We have two days left to get her to do it. I won't be able to stand it if she doesn't."

Two things impressed me right away. The first was that Bob, a former PGA champion and tutor to some of the best professionals in the game, was willing to ask a twenty-eight-year-old sport psychologist to help him. His ego wasn't so big that he couldn't try to learn something from someone with perhaps one percent of his experience in the game. The second was his utter refusal to consider the possibility that this woman was beyond help.

We talked for two hours or so about various approaches that we could try with her. And by the end of the week, she did draw the ball. I trust that she happily hit draws to the end of her days and got her handicap under 30. I suspect, however, that I learned more from Bob Toski that week than she did.

This is the kind of attitude you should look for in a golf professional. When you find one with that attitude, stick with him or her. Don't spoil what he or she is trying to do by going to another teacher and perhaps getting different advice.

YOU CAN MAKE your head a practice range. There is a technique that uses the imagination to fool the mind and body into reacting as if what is in reality nerve-wracking is familiar, safe and comfortable. It's a form of daydreaming that is conscious and purposeful.

Sports psychology has adapted this technique from studies of two natural phenomena: nightmares and nocturnal orgasms. In both cases, nothing is really happening to the individual. He is merely dreaming, of something frightening in the case of nightmares, or of something sexually stimulating in the case of nocturnal emissions. But the dream causes a genuine physical reaction. The body stiffens and trembles with fear from a nightmare, just as it would stiffen and tremble if faced with a genuine fright. The sexually stimulating dream causes a real orgasm.

A golfer can mentally simulate the experience of reaching his goal, whether it be winning a tournament or breaking 100. If he does it vividly enough, he can in effect fool the mind and body into thinking that the experience actually happened. Later, when he actually comes close to that goal on the golf course, he will not experience discomfort or disorientation. He will instead have a sense of déjà vu, a comforting and calming feeling that he has been in this situation before and handled it successfully.

If a golfer tells me he wants to win the U.S. Open, I tell him to try to imagine that experience as vividly as he can. He needs to create, in his brain, all the sensory messages that would bombard him as he actually played the last holes of the Open, in contention to win. He needs to smell the grass and hear the murmur of the crowd. He needs to feel the tackiness of his grips, the way the sweat trickles down his forehead and the churning in his gut. He needs to see the way the rough pinches into the fairways, to see the television towers and to see, in his own mind, his golf ball soaring high against the blue sky and landing on the short grass. He needs to imagine something going wrong, to hear the way the crowd noise changes when a ball kicks into the sand, and to imagine himself taking a bogey but retaining his equilibrium. He needs to imagine hearing a roar from some other part of the course and to imagine his response to a competitor reeling off a string of birdies.

If a golfer tells me his goal is to break 90, I tell him to imagine himself on the way to shooting an 86. Like the professional striving to win the U.S. Open, he would try to simulate all the sensory experiences. He should imagine himself calmly refusing to get distracted when his buddies tell him after nine holes that he's on track to shoot in the eighties. He should imagine staying with his routine and game plan. He should see the shots he will play on all of the final holes, both good and bad.

This technique can be very helpful to professionals who have trouble maintaining a hot round. Sometimes a player finds that whenever he makes two or three birdies on the first few holes, he loses momentum. He can't use that good start as a spring-board to a really low score. One reason is that he doesn't see himself as the kind of player who shoots 70, or 69 at best. When he gets to three under par, he unconsciously believes that he's reached his limit. He starts to look for something bad to happen. He plays defensively.

If this kind of golfer prepares his mind for shooting lower scores, he'll have an easier time staying focused and making even more birdies the next time he gets off to a quick start.

But the technique won't work if your approach to it is per-functory, any more than you would trick your body into a fright reaction simply by saying to yourself, "Okay, there's a burglar coming through my bedroom window." You have to imagine in vivid detail, much as a novelist draws the reader into a setting by describing the sensory experiences of his characters.

Val Skinner used this technique just hours before she won in Atlanta in 1994. Because of rain delays, the players had to finish their Saturday rounds early Sunday morning. Val had several hours before she was supposed to tee off for the final round, in a group with Liselotte Neumann, the leader, and Judy Dicken-son. She went back to her hotel and lay down. She imagined the way her round would go. She could see everything vividly, right down to the colors her opponents would wear. In her daydream round, she was thirteen under par. The holes had a vivid clarity. On one par-three, for instance, she imagined that she almost got a hole-in-one, but the ball lipped out of the cup and she had to settle for a birdie. Her daydream ended as she accepted the winner's check on the 18th green. Then she got up and went to the golf course.

She did not, of course, shoot thirteen under par. Nor did she almost make a hole-in-one. But she made up a two-stroke deficit and won the tournament. Her daydream, she thought, gave her a feeling of serenity that lasted throughout the round. So intently did she feel that she had won the tournament before she started her final round that when it came time to accept the winner's check, she felt a bit deflated. She had a sense that she had been there and done that.

In the evening, before your next important round, make a regular habit of lying down, closing your eyes, and trying this technique. It should help you. It certainly will be more pleasant than pacing around the room and worrying.

22.

What I Learned from
Paul Runyan

....
....
....

A FEW YEARS ago, I was in Toronto to speak to a meeting of 800 teaching golf professionals. I followed Paul Runyan on the schedule.

Paul, who is in his eighties, stood up and began his talk by saying, "I must apologize to each and every one of you."

Every one of the pros came to attention.

"A year ago," Paul went on, "I spoke at your annual meeting and I told you I would work out forty-five to fifty minutes a day, without fail, every day of the year. I'm sorry to tell you that I got lazy two days last year and did not work out. I want you to know that I didn't live up to my commitment, and I promise you that it won't happen again this year."

Everyone in the audience looked startled. Some of them might have thought this was a rhetorical ploy of some kind.

But I knew that it wasn't. He was just telling them the truth about the way Paul Runyan lives his life and the way he honors his commitments.

Doing instructional schools for years with Paul has given me a chance to observe him. He gets up each morning at 5:30. He stretches, exercises, and goes for a substantial walk before breakfast. Then he eats something healthy—oatmeal, perhaps. He's basically a vegetarian.

He gets to the golf course by seven o'clock or so, an hour before the instructional school starts. He goes to the practice green and chips, pitches and putts for forty-five minutes or so. He can drop ten balls in the fringe around a green and get all of them into the hole in less than twenty strokes; he'll chip in more often than he'll fail to get up and down. Then he goes to the range and hits wedges for ten or fifteen minutes, followed by maybe four or five drivers. He's ready to teach.

He teaches until noon, when he goes home and has a light, healthy lunch with Bernice, his wife. Then he teaches again until 4:30. After that, he's likely to want to play nine holes, carrying his own bag. Paul's only concession to age is playing a two-piece ball. As an octogenarian, he's succumbed to the yen for distance that infects most golfers in their teens. His touch around the green is so acute that he can afford to give away the backspin and control most pros get from a balata ball.

After hours, Paul and Bernice still compete in fox-trot contests and cribbage tournaments. They embody an old Satchel Paige aphorism. Someone once asked Paige, the great African-American pitcher who was in his forties before segregation ended and he got to the big leagues, if he could still pitch at that advanced age.

"How old," Paige replied, "would you be if you didn't know how old you was?"

A firm, balanced commitment has been the hallmark of Paul Runyan's life. When he was fourteen or so, he competed in a golf tournament for the first time. He was short and scrawny, and most of the boys in the tournament could drive it 40 yards farther than he could. He reacted by deciding that he would develop a short game so good it would make up for his lack of distance. It did. In his prime, he won tournaments against the likes of Sam Snead, giving away 60 yards off the tee. He was so good around the greens that his nickname was "Little Poison."

Paul's example shows what commitment should mean, and commitment is the final component of a good golfing mentality. To play the best golf you can play, you have to make a healthy, balanced commitment to the game and to improvement.

SOMETIMES, WITH PROFESSIONALS, I find problems of overcommitment. A player is so intent on performing well that he starts to forget that trying harder is not always trying better. And he starts to forget that the game is supposed to be fun.

Mark McCumber, when I started working with him, needed to learn to relax a little. Mark was a fine golfer, but his desire to win and improve was starting to consume him. He was too tense and too serious about the game and life. And he knew it was not helping either his performance on the course or his relationships off it.

"None of us are going to get out of here alive," I told Mark. "You might as well have some fun while you're here."

He had to stop thinking so much about money and titles and start thinking again of golf as the game he just loved to play when he was a kid. He had to stop feeling guilty about easing up on himself a little. I told him that more often than not, good things come to people who stop trying to force them to happen. And good things have indeed come to Mark. He won three times in 1994.

I don't advise people to commit their lives completely and exclusively to golf. That would be like deciding to eat only cookies. It would be bad nutrition. And it would soon spoil your taste for cookies.

This issue arises sometimes when the parents of a youngster ask me for advice. Their child is tearing up the juniors. Her dream is to make millions on the LPGA Tour. So, she reasons, why does she need to study? She should spend all her time honing her golf game.

Well, she needs to study. She could sprain her back getting out of bed some morning and have nothing but her education to support her. Or she could just decide at the age of twenty-two that she's tired of golf and wants to do something else with her life. Studying requires discipline and concentration, two qualities important to anyone.

Some parents, though, are concerned about their child's golf dreams for another reason. They know the odds against success. They want to shield her from disappointment and failure.

I tell them not to worry. Certainly, if a child dreams about becoming a professional golfer, she will encounter disappointment and failure along the way. But why worry about that? People develop pride and find satisfaction, not from doing things that are easy, but from trying things that are difficult, that most people don't even dare to aspire to. I never tell a youngster or anyone else to put aside a dream. Suppose Nick Price had given up on his dreams in 1990, after six winless years? If you give up your dreams, you'll never know if everything might have fallen into place the next week.

The answer for anyone, of any age, who is propelled by a

dream is a balanced commitment. No one should spend all of his time chasing the dream of becoming a great golfer. But during those hours that he sets aside each day to pursue that dream, he has to give golf his undivided attention and energy. And he has to put those hours in every day, regardless of heat, humidity, cold and wind. He has to put them in on the days when he seems stalled on an infinite plateau as well as on days when he feels the gratification of noticeable improvement.

And he needs to realize that commitment need not warp his personality and behavior. Sometimes golfers think they're supposed to be angry and depressed if they have a bad round or a bad tournament. They've been taught that the proper reaction to this kind of misfortune is to get mad and go to the practice tee and beat balls until it gets dark. Then they think they're supposed to brood about their mistakes all night. They think this shows they're committed to the game.

That's not the kind of commitment I'm talking about. For one thing, to flourish on the Tour, a golfer needs the support of friends and family, if not of a spouse. If she wants that, it behooves her to show that she can be an enjoyable human being regardless of what happens on the course.

Some golfers think they should be committed to somehow mastering the game and keeping it in the palm of their hand, as if it were a car or a piece of property that they could own. They can't. They have to recognize that there will be times when they hit the ball beautifully and times when they hit it abominably. And they have to understand that even at their best, they will not come close to mastering the game. Nick Price, as well as he was playing in 1993 or 1994, was perhaps reaching six on a scale of ten, with ten being perfection.

. . .

ON THE OTHER hand, I sometimes run into people who think they can become scratch golfers without making a commitment.

They can't. And I take pride in never saying "can't"!

If you haven't been thinking properly on the golf course, just reading this book and adopting its suggestions can help you. If you have a handicap of 25 and you make up your mind that, henceforth, you will trust your swing when you're on the course, you will follow a sound routine and you will learn to accept your results without getting angry, you can make a quick and noticeable improvement in your scores. You might, for instance, lower your handicap over a summer from 25 to 15 by learning to think well.

But if you want to become a low-handicap golfer, it's not going to be enough simply to read this book, or any other book. You have to make a long-term improvement plan and a commitment more like the one Paul Runyan made. Your plan should include how many times a week you will practice, what you will work on, and for how long. It should include lots of time for short-game practice. Then you must execute that plan.

If someone tells me that he wants to lower his handicap to 5 but he can't find time to practice, I can only tell him that people who consistently play in the mid-70s generally do find time to practice. They get out a few evenings a week after work to hit balls, chip and putt. Or they get to a course early in the morning. They find time at home to work on grip, posture and alignment. They spend a few moments every day visualizing their routines. Most important, they never waste practice time mindlessly hitting balls. They practice with a purpose.

If you want to become a low-handicap golfer, you have to remember what I told Nick Price, Tom Kite, Pat Bradley, and many others about free will. You have the power to make choices. You have the power to think in ways that will help your game. You have the power to make a commitment and keep it.

The happiest people have a sense of commitment in everything they do, whether it's playing golf, running a restaurant or selling hardware. They approach their undertakings with passion.

Golf can give you this happiness whether it's your profession or your hobby. It doesn't matter if you never win a tournament. Golf will challenge you, will give you a chance to test yourself. If you take the ability you have and do the best you can with it, you'll be happy.

No matter what happens, you will find wonderful people who love golf and will be happy to share your commitment with you. They are part of the game's rewards.

In the end, you will realize that you love golf because of what it teaches you about yourself.

Appendix

• A person with great dreams can achieve great things.

• People by and large become what they think about themselves.

• Golfing potential depends primarily on attitude, skill with the wedges and the putter, and how well a golfer thinks. Great golfers are simply ordinary people thinking well and doing extraordinary deeds.

• Free will is a golfer's greatest source of strength and power. Choosing how to think is a crucial decision.

• Golfers who realize their potential generally cultivate the three D's—desire, determination and discipline; the three P's—persistence, patience and practice; and the three C's—confidence, concentration and composure.

• There is no such thing as a golfer playing over his head. A hot streak is simply a glimpse of a golfer's true potential.

• A golfer must train herself in physical technique and then learn to trust what she's trained.

• Before playing any shot, a golfer must lock her eyes and mind into the smallest possible target.

• To score consistently, a golfer must think consistently. A sound, consistent pre-shot routine makes it easier.

• The correlation between thinking well and making successful shots is not 100 percent. But the correlation between thinking badly and unsuccessful shots is much higher.

• Golfers must learn to quiet their minds, stay in the present, and focus tightly on the next shot to be played.

• The loss of focus on four or five shots a round makes the difference between great golf and mediocre golf.

• A golfer must learn to enjoy the process of striving to improve the short game.

• Attitude makes a great putter.

• As ball-striking skills improve, it becomes a greater challenge to love putting and the short game and to maintain a positive attitude toward them.

• It is more important to be decisive than to be correct when preparing to play any golf shot, particularly a putt.

• Confidence is crucial to good golf. Confidence is simply the aggregate of the thoughts you have about yourself.

• A golfer cannot let the first few holes, shots, or putts determine his thinking for the rest of the round.

• A golfer should strive to be looser, freer, and more confident with every hole. This will combat the tendency to get tighter, more careful, and more doubtful.

• Being careful, tightening up, and trying to steer the ball will likely cause disaster. Good golfers gain control over the ball by feeling that they are giving up control.

• Golfers need selective memories, retaining the memory of great shots and forgetting bad ones. Selective memory helps a golfer grow in confidence as he gains experience and skill.

• Golf is a game played by human beings. Therefore, it is a game of mistakes. Successful golfers know how to respond to mistakes.

• Golfers must learn to love the challenge when they hit a ball into the rough, trees, or sand. The alternatives—anger, fear, whining, and cheating—do no good.

• Patience is a cardinal virtue in golf. To improve, a golfer must learn how to wait for practice and good thinking to bear fruit.

• At night, a golfer can program her mind with great expectations. But she must throw them away when she steps onto the first tee.

• On the first tee, a golfer must expect only two things of himself: to have fun, and to focus his mind properly on every shot.

• Players with great attitudes constantly monitor their thinking and catch themselves as soon as it begins to falter.

• A good competitor never allows herself to intensely dislike another player. She might be paired with her for an important round.

• The quality of a golfer's practice is more important than the quantity, particularly for better golfers.

• If a golfer chooses to compete, he must choose to believe that he can win. Winners and losers in life are completely self-determined, but only the winners are willing to admit it.

• Courage is a necessary quality in all champions. But an athlete cannot be courageous without first being afraid.

• In sport, the bad news for the present champion is that tomorrow is a new day, when the competition starts again from scratch. But that's the good news for everyone else.

• On the course, golfers must have the confidence of a champion. But off the course, champions must remember that they are not more important than anyone else.

Acknowledgments

I HAVE BEEN BLESSED WITH A LOT OF PEOPLE TO THANK.

I've had the opportunity to associate with many of the greatest golfers and golf teachers of this era. Most of them are mentioned in the text of this book. I want to thank them all. Without their contributions, my work would be a laboratory exercise.

Three players in particular—Tom Kite, Brad Faxon, and Val Skinner—took extra time to share thoughts and experiences that make this a more informative book, and I am grateful to them.

I also want to thank Dr. Bruce Gansneder for his hours of tireless help with golf psychology research over a period of many years.

I owe great debts as well to my father, Guido Rotella, and to my brothers, Drs. Jay and Guy Rotella, for hours of listening and discussion. Each of them read the manuscript and made valuable suggestions.

I also wish to thank Tony Carroll, Steve Grant, Bruce Stewart, and Rod Thompson, all of whom read this as a work in progress and contributed questions and ideas for its improvement.

I am grateful to Bob Carney and Andy Nusbaum for their encouragement over the years. Dominick Anfuso at Simon & Schuster and Rafe Sagalyn, my literary agent, helped conceive the book and helped me find Bob Cullen as a collaborator. My special thanks go to them.